CINDY H

The Sticky Book of Stuckness

WHAT'S HOLDING YOU BACK?

Rᵉthink

First published in Great Britain in 2020 by Rethink Press
(www.rethinkpress.com)

Cover image © Ольга Калиниченко | Dreamstime.com

Back cover and p163 photography by Mary Doggett:
https://ettphotography.co.uk

Contents

For my Mom and Dad and loving husband, Nicholas

Introduction

I always say there are two types of people. There are the 'bottom-of-the-sea' people. And the 'top-of-the-sea' people.

The bottom-of-the-sea people are the artists, philosophers, writers, musicians, healers. The deep thinkers, reflectors, spiritually inclined. They are the recorders of life.

Then there are the top-of-the-sea people. Skimming along the surface, they just get on with doing, for they are the doers.

One group of people is as important as the other. It is the job of the bottom-of-the-sea people to help the top-of-the-sea people drop into themselves and discover more, while the job of the top-of-the-sea people is to persuade the bottom-of-the-sea people to lighten up and get things done.

I most definitely am a bottom-of-the-sea person.

My mother tells the story of when, aged five years old, I asked her, 'Why don't people say on the outside what they are saying inside?' It was then I started to own who I am. Like many intuitives, I am creative, spiritual and often otherworldly. I see everything as energy. Always have.

Working with people – individuals and groups – on a personal level has always been a good fit for me. With over thirty years as a transformational coach, shifting perspectives and opening the doors of awareness, I have helped many connect to the calm found underneath the stormy seas. Able to intuit destructive and limiting patterns, my clients and students shift perspective. Seeing the bigger picture, they discover more of who they are. Changing energy patterns is key to personal growth.

But being good at the bottom-of-the-sea stuff often makes the top-of-the-sea doing more of a challenge. I had patterns which blocked my progress. The sticky strands of stuckness were wrapping around me. Annoyed and frustrated that for some reason, every so often (usually just when I was really making headway), all would stop, for the life of me, I couldn't see my part in creating the sticky stuckness.

My area of frustration tended to focus on my writing. I didn't have an issue with completion. It was just that once I'd finished with something, I would forget about it. Turn my attention elsewhere. Which is useless. It is like planting a seed, watching it grow, and then just as it fruits, taking your attention elsewhere and planting another seed. Not a path I suspect a top-of-the-sea person would take.

And then out of nowhere, this book was born, formed by a riptide of fuelled inspiration. I felt I was surfing, and my job? Keeping balance and riding that wave. The energy flowing through me was tangible. It has changed my life.

How did it do that? I saw myself. Clearly saw the energetic patterns which had blocked me time and time again. And once we see something, really see it, we can't go back. We have to go forward.

I describe people as balls of energy. It is by seeing energetic patterns that we grow our awareness, helping us to shift negating ones and fuelling those that are supportive. But the trick is to see what we are doing. Take it from me with over forty years in the personal growth field, we can be quite invisible, making it difficult to see ourselves. Which explains how over and over again, we suffer uncomfortable feelings caused by behavioural patterns.

You too may know the limitation of blocked energy, for I am sure stuckness is a universal problem. Who doesn't know the discomfort of not being able to get from here to there or stumbling along the path? When our energetic process is blocked, frustration builds and negativity increases, feeding self-doubt and fear, fuelling low self-esteem. Stuck energy is uncomfortable. It's living life on a low ebb while we're wanting to break free. Why? Because there is more to us waiting in the wings. Ready to take flight.

It matters not where the stuck patterns lie. For some, it's relationship patterns, while for others it may be purely a matter of sustaining energy flow. Stuckness comes in all shapes and sizes.

Using metaphors and analogies and simple, readable concepts, my book brings into focus how we hold ourselves back. Describing three mindsets and thirty actions which hinder progress, it opens the eyes of you, the reader, to where you are now. Some you may not relate to, while others will most definitely hit the nail on the head, which is exactly what you need for building new structures.

Which of these mindsets can you relate to?

Lost in thought – a powerful mind inhibited by excessive thought will curtail creative energy. Instead of flowing outwards to the next manifestation point, your energy gets sucked up into the whirlpool of the mind, making it difficult for you to take action.

Up in the air – here there is a disconnect. Unable to sustain an energy pattern, you'll find it easier to float free, allowing ideas to happen in your imagination, but not in the reality surrounding you.

Sidestepping – with this mindset, energy gets stuck in a holding pattern, shuttering and unable to find direction. The pattern focuses on stopping the shutter by either changing the energy or abandonment.

The Sticky Book of Stuckness lets the light in. Once we see what we are doing, the game is up. I saw in myself the energy pattern that had blocked me for years, and in that realisation, my wings soared with future possibilities. This book can do the same for you.

With every journey, you first need to know where you are so you can know where you are going. If you focus only on your goal, your dream is futile. It is easy to dream, but much more of a challenge to get from here to there. If I wanted to go to London and needed to figure out how to get there, how inept would all my planning be if I never thought to consider my starting point or had no awareness of how to reconfigure when I lost my direction?

The Sticky Book of Stuckness is not a how-to book, but a where-you-are book. As with any awareness-raising guidance, its aim is to shed light on how you trip yourself up, lose momentum, go off track or change track all together – get, in a word, stuck.

When we're entangled in the stuckness web, our energy flow always suffers. We lose hope, confusion increases, fuelling fear, and we abandon what we intended or needed to do. This creates an energy block, strangling and inhibiting life force.

And we all do it to ourselves. Who doesn't struggle with momentum? We are creative energy with the ability to bring thought into reality. But how many of us don't have a cupboard full of abandoned projects, great ideas with fantastic potential that never quite made it from there to here? Who hasn't suffered the disappointment of discomfort and self-doubt because the dream keeps moving just out of reach?

We all have different ways and different reasons for blocking ourselves, allowing those sticky strands to wrap us into discomfort. But we also have an innate ability to improve energy flow. Get ourselves going. Feel the joy of creative movement. Embrace potential.

By portraying behaviour as energy, I want to make it easier to go below the surface of the problem, gaining necessary insight and awareness to set free stuck energy and direct it into more productive and life-enhancing patterns. With greater awareness, you will learn to recognise not only your patterns, but also those of people you know. You'll take away judgement of yourself and others, expanding perspective to help all to see the bigger picture, offering insight and improving communication. For when you look deeper inside yourself, you will be that much closer to your Heart.

An open Heart recognises that we are all made of the same stuff, but have a unique pattern making us, us. We all have innate skills, thoughts, ideas, love, wisdom, practicalities (and so much more) waiting to be shared.

The Sticky Book of Stuckness throws back the curtains of confusion and allows the light of awareness to flood in. For it is only when we can see something that we can change it. When we step into the creative flow, our Heart sings. Unobstructed vitality and life force step up to the plate and diminish fear, allowing everyone to benefit.

It is imperative to wellbeing that creative energy flows. Freeing yourself allows healthy creative energy momentum. Stepping out of stuckness means stepping up into you.

If we could all see ourselves as balls of energy and without judgement work towards untangling the web of stuckness, how much better would life be?

PART ONE
WHERE ARE YOU NOW?

ONE

Everything Is Energy

It's said that the best way to write a book is to write what you know. I guess this one will tell you a lot about me, but I don't believe I'm any different than you. I don't think anyone escapes the discomfort of being caught in the tangled sticky strands of stuckness.

For some, it may be an occasional occurrence, like trying to get a report written and suddenly finding themselves judging every word, getting caught up in the what ifs, feeling a strong urge to clean the house right now, or perhaps just disappearing deep inside themselves and not wanting to come out. For others, stuckness may be more of a challenge, the strands wrapping them up and seemingly leaving no possible way to get from here to there.

But how amazing do we feel when we are enthused, involved, committed, challenged, giving birth to a new idea, project or lifestyle change? Our energy flows, we are moving forward and engaged in the process of doing, becoming, partaking. And it feels so good.

Simply put, herein lies the clue – when our energy moves (as energy must), we feel good. When it is blocked, it's not so good. In fact, it's darn uncomfortable and limiting.

We are all made from the same source, just with our own unique patterns, so how you get stuck may not be how I do. But what matters is not so much the how, but more the need to understand and see clearly *what* we are doing when we put the brakes on, creating an internal traffic jam, and what we are doing to resume forward movement.

Movement is essential to wellbeing. If we can recognise the what, when and how of the occasions we allow the sticky strands of stuckness to pull us into their web, blocking the vitality of self, then we can step back into the good-feeling flow of creative energy, moving forward.

With over thirty years' experience working with both individuals and groups as a transformational coach, I have travelled into many a mind. This has given me a gift of learning about how we tick as human beings, and when we do not, how to reboot, fuel, get focused and get going. But even more importantly, I have learned that when we're invisible to ourselves, we cannot see the patterns and habits of emotional responses, self-doubt, lack of confidence, low self-esteem. It is these unseen patterns and behaviours which allow the sticky web to entangle us like a spider ensnares a fly, and before we know it, we are not going anywhere. We are stuck, blocked, living in a low ebb of frustration and depleted energy.

Getting from here to there

To do whatever you feel you want to do, to get there from here, first you have to see exactly where you are.

Imagine you want to map out a road trip. Getting to your destination is your goal, but how can you possibly do that if you have no idea where you are? At the same time, you need to see when you lose your direction so you can reconfigure, putting you back on course. Seeing where you are is truly the beginning of the journey.

Being invisible to ourselves makes it hard to see not only what we are doing or not doing, but also the deep-seated habits which create dams within, stopping the flow and the essence of us.

Ask any creative how they feel when their energy is flowing and they're likely to tell you it's joyful, like surfing the perfect wave. But when it's not? Intensely uncomfortable. I am in flow now, so I've written these words with ease, but I too can step out of the flow into wearing the concrete blocks of self-doubt or judgement. To say that I have seen a lot of my own stuck patterns manifest throughout the writing of this book is truly an understatement. But my seeing has shifted my energy immeasurably.

That is what I truly hope for you.

Energy must flow

The premise to all my transformational work (in the many ways it's expressed) is that I see everything as energy. You are a ball of energy. I am a ball of energy. As are our thoughts, feelings, ideas, confusions, struggles, achievements, joys, sorrows, misunderstandings, pain, discoveries (the list is endless). And everything around us is the same – energy. Everything. Not only my thoughts or the movement of my fingers as I write, but also the keys they touch.

Energy must move, and when its flow is blocked, a pressure builds up inside, wanting to burst the dam. But we humans have become so clever at ignoring or displacing discomfort. We excuse it away or blame life.

I am sure all of us know when we are on fire, blazing with energy and life force. It doesn't have to be as dramatic as that, but when our energy is flowing in a healthy, productive manner, we are not only able to get on with things, we also have a smile on our face and, more importantly, in our Heart.

Let's face it, we are living in a challenging time. We haven't been good carers and keepers of the great being we walk upon, and now, like ourselves, it is suffering in the sticky web of stuckness. It is trying to realign as energy needs to move. Hence flooding, earthquakes, storms.

In my twenties, I taught art classes in my kitchen to small groups of children aged from seven to ten years old. I asked the children to draw a picture of a feeling. An eight-year-old boy drew a picture of a volcano.

I asked him, 'What feeling is that?' His answer?

'It's the Earth's way of getting angry.'

Blocked energy seeks release. We too can get angry, negative, depressed, fearful when we are no longer in alignment with our natural flow of energy. This anger is seen not only in the Earth around us, but in its inhabitants as well.

Yes, that sticky web of stuckness has a lot to answer for.

But imagine if we all opened our eyes, letting the invisibility of our self emerge into the light of awareness. If we created healthier energy patterns – positive, connecting, loving. How much better would we all feel?

Where are you?

Knowing where you are is a key component to all that you do and hope to do. How are you in yourself? Are you even in yourself?

What does it feel like to be you at this very moment in time? How are you? What's going on in your head? Spinning plates with too much to do? Focused on keeping everything up in the air – stressed? Locked away? Thinking about what you are thinking about? Thinking only of everyone else, forgetting about you? Is the inside of you louder than the world around you?

And what about the feelings department? Pesky things, those feelings. Have you shut the door so you can better manage? Or are you drowning in the tsunami of yourself?

What about the physical? How are you? Not a report on your health, back pains, bunions, physical limitations, but how much energy do you have? Is it constant? Are you lacking? Do you have so much that it is hard to manage, never letting you take a back seat and allow someone else to drive the rocket?

Are you struggling? Frustrated? Feeling like you can't get here from there? Or not even bothering to try? Maybe you are in a great place. Feeling creative, productive, connected and comfortable with yourself.

Wherever you are, step away from your judgement and take what I call an energetic snapshot. But how do you do that?

I live in England and my family of origin lives in the United States, so I don't get to see them that often. One of the things I do when we are together is to make sure I'm present with them. I take an energetic snapshot and place it in my Heart.

I remember clearly doing that with my dad. I was hypnotising him, and the image I carry is him relaxed, feet up on the lazy boy. I was present with him and saw what was, and I captured it. He is gone from this world now, but in my Heart, I hold the nowness of that moment.

When we take an energetic snapshot of ourselves, we do a similar thing, being aware of where we are in one moment. If I take one of me right now, my energy is focused, directed towards what I'm writing while at the same time receiving insights. I feel fantastic, alive, creative, full of possibilities and probabilities. In a word, grateful – I'm grateful for being where I am right now.

I also know how difficult and frustrated energy feels when it is not flowing. Probably the biggest frustration of my life was wanting to write, but at the same time pulling away from doing so. If I cast my mind back to the before energy pattern, I always felt like I could get so far, and then everything, be it encouragement, opportunities, health, drive, continuity, would suddenly stop. Fall away.

It drove me absolutely crazy. Why? Because I could not figure out why the pattern of my life was so start-stop.

What changed? The change happened in the same way I am asking you to change. I stopped focusing on where I wanted to go, planning, hoping, fuelling, and instead bit the bullet and saw where I was. Where was I? Stuck. Energy must flow, and if it isn't, it means it is blocked somewhere.

Clearing energy traffic jams

In England, with lots of cars and relatively few major road systems, even one or two inches of snow can slow traffic down, often to a complete standstill. Why? For a number of reasons, but a common one is that it only takes a few people to abandon their cars to lead to complete gridlock. And I know in myself, I've often created my stuckness through abandonment – being a creative person, I would be off and running to do something else before completing the first goal.

When we abandon our goals, we move away and leave them. Then, just like on the roads of England, a traffic jam builds elsewhere.

Everything is energy, and if any little avenue of yourself is blocked, that will affect the energy flow in other areas.

My husband is an acupuncturist, and the way I like to describe acupuncture is to imagine that the body's wellbeing is like a huge road system. A healthy flow of energy heals and sustains wellbeing. But if something is not working as it should, it clogs up the roads. Energy slows, creating more problems. My uneducated take on acupuncture is that redirecting the flow of energy helps release blockages. When the pressure is off, energy will find a healthy flow once again.

When energy is stuck, we don't feel so good. That's why it is important to take stock of where we are. It is through the negatives that we are able to see where our energy is trapped, stored but not being using, neglected, undervalued. By creating an awareness of our energetic patterns without judgement, we are ready to start that journey of releasing it.

Take it from me, it makes little sense to focus only on where you want to be. It helps, as desires to achieve a goal fuel motivation, but if you don't have enough energy to get there, what you are doing is only hoping.

It's like setting off on a long car journey without taking into account that not only do you not have enough petrol, but you have no money to buy any. You could hop in the car and go until the petrol ran out, but how foolish would that be? An unrealistic adventure. Or at best, short lived. Just like a car with a full tank and working well, we too are able to travel far when energy flows.

I know what it feels to be stuck, but I also know what it feels to be unstuck. Use the advice in this book as a microscope into your energy system. Sometimes, we all need help to magnify what we cannot see with the naked eye. It is my hope that my words will help you see the patterns of stuckness better, and in a not-too-painful way.

Being invisible to ourselves, we tend to react to the frustration of life by focusing on what is not happening rather than seeing clearly our part in destructive or limiting patterns. We are all adept at holding, blocking, storing, excusing or ignoring anything we don't want to look at or cannot see. My aim is to shed light into the pattern of you at this moment. Light in darkness brings clarity, creating visibility, helping you see how you do, indeed, create the traffic jams of the Spirit.

TWO

No Judgement Allowed

I always ask two things of the people who attend any of my Personal Awareness workshops:

- If you have judgements, please leave them in the bucket just outside the room. On leaving, feel free to retrieve them. Otherwise, I am happy to empty the bucket later.

- Be open to experience.

Why? Because without any preconceived ideas or judgements of ourselves or others, we can just hang out with one another and learn.

You are entering my world, and in my world, no one is better than the next. We all have bits which work really well, and bits in need of improvement. But life is a process.

When viewing life through the dulled lens of judgement, we do not totally engage. We have decided already what is and is not open to experience. There is a place for judgement, but not right now. Certainly not against yourself.

Why do we judge?

When we are quick to judge others, it is self-protection, deciding what is dangerous, worth our while, of value. But while we are busy judging in our heads, without even knowing it, we have drawn a line between the possibility of experience and what we will accept.

Everything is energy. Get used to me hammering that home. In my mind, it's the only way to think. And the energy of judgement has a valued place, best used for weighing up information. Which is the better contract? What are the pros and cons of buying this house or another? Who is best suited for the job? What are they bringing to the table that suits our needs? Personal decisions made from a logical perspective of examining information. No different than what happens in a courtroom. This is when it is essential to stick with the energy of judgement. Judgement, like the old-fashion scales of justice, does the weighing and measuring.

But when we mix a dollop of sensibility and rational thought with the emotional soup, it changes in purpose. Skipping the information gathering, the weighing and measuring, we prejudge. We believe we know who someone is or what is going to happen. By skipping an essential part of the judgement process, we end up blocking the experience waiting to happen.

Take this moment in time. If you had judged my book by the cover and decided it was codswallop, you and I would not be having this Heart to Heart. When we are quick to judge first (prejudge), we remove ourselves from the experience. We have already decided what is, judging away new experiences. Which can leave us in a bit of a quandary.

Why? Quite simply, how can you know the value of something if you have no experience of it? You can't.

The cost of prejudging

When we're quick to judge, whether it's ideas, opportunities, situations and/or people, we create a judgement barrier around us. We use judgement as protection, much like a moat surrounding a castle.

When attendees at my workshops wear the dimmed lenses of judgement, they pull back. Not only do they have a reinforced wall beyond their moat, but they have taken up the drawbridge as well. Now all they can do is sit and watch from one of the castle windows, seeing only what they have judged to be true. Why? Because they still have the glasses on – the ones with the dimmed lenses – and they're looking out at the world as they are sure it is. They're not participating in the energy flow for all. Hence, at my workshops, any judgements are best dumped in the bucket.

But why do we sit in the window seat of judgement? Interesting question, that. The energy of judgement is found on the left side of the brain – our analytical side. No feelings in that landscape.

When we are quick to judge, we are protecting ourselves from feeling. While busy judging others, we have no space to wonder what they think of us and, with focus on the outside for a few brief moments, we bounce away from self-judgement. By judging others, we get away from the inner critic.

I call this inner critic our troll – the big, bad guy inside our heads who's always giving us a hard time. Pointing out mistakes, reinforcing failure and fuelling low self-esteem. No wonder we hang out in the protected tower. But we're not only keeping everyone else out, keeping change away, we're also, and maybe more importantly, keeping our feelings at bay. Like the sign on a boy's tree house saying, 'No girls allowed', but this one says, 'No feelings allowed'.
Judgement shuts the door on feelings. Hanging out in the tower serves two purposes. No one gets in and it

keeps the mind busy, so it doesn't have to feel. Nothing stirs.

But why would we do that? Step away from feelings? They are the barometers of life. They clue us in. Tell us what is going on at a deep level and connect us to the riches of life. For even in despair and grief, there are treasures to be found. Another thing you may want to get used to me saying is that there is positive and negative in all things. When quick to judge, we see only lack, missing out on the bounty.

What about self-judgement? Usually when we're prone to judging things outside ourselves, we are also pretty adept at giving ourselves a hard time. Just as we judge others as being not up to scratch, we believe we aren't.

Inside or outside judgement as a defence mechanism is not a comfortable energy and blocks experience. Locked up in such a small tower of self, we make sure everything stays the same. But we need newness to grow, to change.

Leaving judgement at the door

If we carry any judgements, we need to leave them outside the door. In that way, we can learn from one another. Be open to experience.

Sitting there in a tower, absorbed in the critical mind, isn't going to get anyone going, but it will keep us stuck.

While we're judging another, we of course assume we are right. This narrow banner in thinking keeps the truth at bay.

To step out of stuckness, we need to embrace the truth, the whole truth and nothing but the truth of where we are. How do we support stuckness? We will only find those answers if we open our mind to self-awareness, are able to see the habitual patterns in thought and deed that block the energy of wellbeing.

I had no idea when I sat down to write this book what would happen to me while doing what I'd always wanted to do. I had no idea how my energy would shift into more productive, sustaining patterns in a short time. How it would affect my vitality, confidence, visibility. The joy I would feel as I was doing what I had been born to do. I'd had glimpses of my potential, but I am so much more than those brief curtain twitchings of the self. And each day, I'm shining brighter than the day before.

Why? Because everything is energy, and when we release the strands which hold us back, we step out of stuckness.

Lower the drawbridge

But none of this would have happened if I'd stayed safe within the patterns that held me back. I had to embrace self-honesty to grow self-awareness. It was only by seeing where I truly was, like light shining into the darkness, that I could gain the awareness of how I fuelled frustration. No one was doing it to me. It had nothing to do with lack of time. Lack of money. Not knowing how or what to write. No. To embrace who I am and evolve, I had to let go of judgement. The judgement of myself.

There is no place for that demeaning and limiting way of thinking – thinking about you. You are, after all, just an energy pattern. Not a failure. Your pattern at the moment may not be supporting a healthy energy flow, but that is OK. When you step out of judgement, you step into possibility. Embracing change, you'll find energy flows.

If you are still carrying any judgements about this book and the fact you are reading it, lower the drawbridge, come out and join me in the creative field of the mind. It's just the other side of the moat. Don't be afraid to feel. Feeling without judgement allows you to check in and check out what you are doing. It allows you to make yourself uncomfortable as well, which is the only way to step into that lovely productive flow of the creative you.

No judgement allowed in this book. If you feel the need to pick it up out of the bucket after you've read the book, feel free to do so. But do it with the knowledge that there is a part of you wanting to shut down again.

Busy judging others, you will miss out on what you need to see and hear, only noticing how much you judge yourself.

Unless you are willing to open up and, without judgement, see clearly the energetic snapshot of where you are right now, you will sacrifice the very impulse drawing you towards my words, my thoughts and change. Judgement keeps the mind busy, so it doesn't have to feel. Step up and step out of stuckness. Allow your energy to flow. Moving energy feels good, so allow it to begin.

THREE

The Cloak Of Invisibility

Just beyond this chapter lies my list of thirty stuck-nesses, broken down into the three mindsets that support them. I have no doubt there are many more, and in fact more pop into my head daily, but for now let's keep it manageable.

I urge you not to jump ahead and delve into the stuck-ness you feel best reflects your holding pattern. Stay with me. Think of this book like the musical scoring of a symphony. Ignoring its natural progression, jumping forward to the easy, interesting or more familiar, you will miss out on the full effect of the gift of the piece – the feeling it gives.

Similarly, the advice I share in this book is a process. So rein in any urge to rush it; instead, plod along beside me. The feelings you'll encounter will make the experience of stuckness recognition more profound. Why? Because you'll achieve a deeper resonance and feel it more. Just as each note in a symphony leads the orchestra to the next, so too does each page prompt awareness and desire to change the pattern. I urge you to stick with the plan.

Seeing ourselves

It is quite simple. With judgement out of the way, all we have to do is see where we are. Release the sticky strands of the stuckness web and allow energy to move. Well, I say it's quite simple, but actually seeing the patterns of our life can be tricky. Why?

Let's talk about the cloak of invisibility.

Why is it so much easier to see what everyone else should do than it is to see what we should be or are doing? Or who we are?

As energy, we are reliant on the mirroring from others to help us see ourselves. This strange conundrum is best explained by imagining we are all born tucked up safely inside a cloak of invisibility. A survival camouflage. Much like young animals blending into their environment until they are strong enough and ready to step out.

As our eyes focus, we look out into the world. First for safety, making the connection with mom and dad, then with curiosity. There's so much to see, hear, smell, touch and taste. All is new and confusing.

As we can only see out, we need the connection of love to reassure us that we are OK. Think of the funny faces and cooing voices which we tend to use with a newborn. The baby learns to copy what they see. If we smile, they smile. If we are stern, they soon learn they are in danger of a reprimand, and a displeased look and voice means they've done something they shouldn't have. And we are all reliant from a very early age on others to reflect back who we are at us. We see out. Not in.

This explains why we are concerned about what other people think of us, wanting the smiles not the frowns to mirror our self-worth. We have learned that a smile is a reward for being good, so it makes us smile – inside and out. It is difficult to truly see ourselves other than as a reflection from those around us. But until we wake from this ingrained pattern, we will always feel invisible. Not to everyone else, but to ourselves, which makes it really hard to see where we are and even harder to see who we are.

Who is Cindy Hurn?

Years ago, struggling with the question 'Who is Cindy Hurn?', I had a bright idea to make it an advert and place it on the side of a local vintage tour bus. There, travelling around the city, usually at under 10 miles an hour, was a two-foot by three-foot sign asking 'Who is Cindy Hurn?' It caused a lot of stir as everyone started to ask the question. Some interesting stories came back to me.

Think about it – it is a huge question to ask yourself (never mind having it travel around the city for five years). This bit of advertising really threw me for a loop. Why? Because although I could see a lot of myself, I was finding it difficult to give a simple answer. I remember being caught up in the question. Not only was I asking it, but it was in the air around me.

One day, while sitting at the traffic lights, confused and concerned about who I was, all of a sudden, I saw 'Who is Cindy Hurn?' appear perfectly framed in the side window of my car. What a shock. The tour bus had simply pulled up alongside me at the lights – but talk about thoughts made manifest!

Who are you?

When you ask yourself that question, it will get you thinking. It is not that you can't think of all the things you are – writer, trainer, radio show presenter, wife, therapist etc – but who exactly are *you*? And that, my friends, is the invisible bit.

When we start to figure out us, we are putting our feet on the path of awareness, becoming more visible bit by bit as the cloak of invisibility shifts and we see more of who we are. Looking through the eyes of self-awareness, we lose dependency on the feedback of others.

But it is a process. A path. The more we tread this path, the more we uncover. The more it reveals.

Our habitual nature

If we can't see ourselves, how do we know we are stuck? Good question. Part of our innate invisibility is our habitual nature, which is repeated behaviour eventually slipping into a habit. A habit is a neural path shooting energy from one point to the other, so we don't have to think about doing it. A good design, really, as it frees thinking for other new avenues of thought.

Take driving a car as an example. When you're a beginner, everything you do in the car is preceded by conscious thoughts. How do I do this? Check the mirror; put it in gear; press on the accelerator; oops – check my speed. Will I fit it in that parking space? A beginner driver can find it exhausting being so aware.

But then one day, while driving, you find yourself thinking about something else. The 'how to' of driving has slipped into the habit department. Part of you is still aware, but not consciously unless there is danger or a decision to be made.

That's the plus of repeating an action – it just becomes what we do habitually. But that can be a negative. To change a behaviour, we have to see it. Remember that cloak? It not only hides us from us, it also makes it difficult to see what we are doing to ourselves.

This is where the value of feelings comes in. Discomfort, no matter how unpleasant it may be, is actually a tap on your shoulder. Take stock. What are you doing? What patterns have you fallen into? Do they serve you? Feelings prod pattern behaviour, like stirring a stagnant pond aerates it, awakening life, promoting growth.

Stuckness is all about energy flow. The pattern of that flow. Remember my layperson's view on road systems? If someone further up the road has broken down, run out of gas, everyone behind them will be affected. If the road is blocked, shut down energy needs to reroute. Getting here to there is now more of an issue. Frustration builds.

Isn't that why you are reading this book?

Listen to your frustration

Frustration is a great energy if we acknowledge what it is trying to tell us. With frustration, the energy battles for release. It's often so uncomfortable that we move further back into ourselves, away from the battle – the Spirit resigns. But that doesn't solve the problem. In fact, all it does is create others. Productive energy is healthy energy.

Own frustration. Which is different than accepting it. What is it saying to you? Let it lift the hem of your invisibility cloak, allowing the essence of you to shine through.

We have to be honest with ourselves to change and to grow. Bite a few bullets. Without judgement (we left that in the bucket at the start of the last chapter), it really doesn't hurt so much. And the growth far outweighs the discomfort of owning destructive behaviours.

To map out the journey, knowing where you are is key. Let the feelings of stuckness help create the visibility of self. It doesn't matter where you are; it's just a point at which to begin.

When I set about writing this book, like all creatives, I let information drop down in me. Taking out my ideas notepad, I wrote the word 'stuckness', drawing a circle around it, and listed every stuckness I knew or had come across. Without thought, thirty stucknesses made it on to the page. Then I just wrote about each one. My aim was to give a visual interpretation to the energy patterns of stuckness. If we can see where we are...well, you know how the rest goes.

The journey has begun.

PART TWO

THE THREE MINDSETS
OF STUCKNESS

I feel stuck
Doing the same old thing
going no where exhausted. No aim
empty. fed up with everyone.
but don't change very noisy
need your advise help.
Sam is doing shitl.
No friends. family useless.
No power!

FOUR
Lost In Thought

When I sat down to write this chapter, I was a bit stumped. Of the three stuckness mindsets, lost in thought is the one I least naturally gravitate towards and identify with. This by no means indicates I have everything sussed and avoid galloping thoughts whisking me away. No. It is just I am much more of a feeling type of person. Being intuitive, I avoid the trap of overthinking by responding to my inner directive. My feelings are my thoughts.

This is a book on stuckness, so guess what? I got stuck. Yep. Lost in thought.

The wonderful gift of self-awareness, especially if you're writing a book on it, is that it teaches you. As your awareness is the light you hold to show others the way, it makes perfect make sense that if you can't relate to it yourself, you are pretty much in the dark and no one will benefit. There I was thinking I couldn't relate to the stuckness list in this chapter and the lesson began. Lost in thought, I started to feel self-doubt and became over-critical of my writing, creating my own writers' block.

Then, as will always happen when we get stuck, my energy flow backed up. Negativity set in, and as it did, I pulled further and further away from my writing. Which really affected my energy levels. I was exhausted and weakened. No longer catching the wave, I felt stranded, standing still on my surfboard. Stuck on the flats, I wasn't going anywhere and felt frustrated, low and hopeless. Stuckness doesn't feel good, especially when it's fed with self-doubt and negativity.

That was until...I realised where I was. Just like the beginning of any journey, I first had to know where I was. Otherwise, how could I map it out? Yes, I had been lost in thought. Thinking more than doing. Not pleasant, but a necessary place to visit so I could truly understand the power of thought stopping forward movement. Experience the challenge of recognising that although I was stuck in the sand, I could easily pick up my surfboard and step back into the water. I just had to override all the self-negating thoughts.

Which is easier said than done.

Let's face it, thoughts are powerful. They are meant to be, for it is this powerful energy that fuels the direction of life. But at times, instead of going forward, we hesitate, overthink, judge, fuel anxiety or self-doubt, and can easily end up caught in all kinds of thought-loops. Much like being on a roundabout unable to exit, round and round we go.

When we spend too much time in our heads (thinking rather than doing), we are hanging out in the inner world. Which is a grand place for stimulating imagination to come up with new ideas, problem solve or figure out our next step. But when we are not using our energy, power or movement in the world around us, guess what? We end up stuck. Which, by the very nature of the beast, fuels judgement and fear, supporting low self-esteem and lack of confidence.

When lost in thought, we just keep repeating patterns of thinking. Nothing new gets in. And as with all stuckness, change needs to happen. Something needs releasing to shift the stuckness strand which is holding us down. Wrapped up in thought. That thread has entangled us.

How do we know if it is our thoughts turned inward which need shifting? How do we know when we are using thought power to make us powerless in the doing world? Inhibiting effectiveness, relationships, wellbeing?

Simple. If the inner world is louder than the world around us, there is a good chance that's where we are putting our energy. Because we are using our energy to fuel doubt, fear, lack of self-worth, judgement of self or others, we feel the deficit in our day-to-day world. We can't be bothered. It's all too much. We're focusing on what is wrong with us...

Imagine thought like a vast sea. It may not be a bad thing to go for a dip or a paddle. After all, we have the ability to think, reflect, analyse, imagine, invent for good purpose. But if we are out over our heads and there is no boat nearby, then we have a problem. That vast sea will suck us down. And that is when it gets tricky.

As energy balls (which we are), we have 100% energy to draw from. Using 90% for overthinking leaves only 10% left. Which is very little energy to shift us and get us moving.

This is when living in our head with only thoughts as company becomes an issue, a problem. Caught on that roundabout, we have no release. Our thoughts can become difficult. Negative. Which will affect wellbeing.

Everything is energy so everything is connected. But with only our own thoughts for company, it can get lonely. We miss out on not only the input of other people, but also – and more importantly – our own input, our potential, our life. We miss out on us in our life. With nothing new entering the roundabout, there is no chance of renewal or growth. In other words, everything stays the same. While the amazing waits just off that darn roundabout.

With my list of thirty stucknesses, I have isolated ten which pertain to being lost in thought. I have to say the challenge of this did get me stuck on the roundabout for a while (yes, again), but then I took the leap I needed to get off it and just let my awareness grow as I compiled the lists.

It is normal to go in and out of stuckness. It only becomes an issue when we remain caught in its sticky web. Struggling to go forward. Awareness is key. Always.

Give the list a read. Some stucknesses may ring true for you more than others. They may even provide an aha moment of insight, blowing back the cloak of invisibility. Helping you to take action. Getting you moving forward, and hopefully gaining deeper understanding of those around you as well.

Fear of failure

This is a two-sided issue. When we are stuck because of an underlying anxiety that we have to get everything right, we tend to:

- Drive ourselves forward, using way too much energy to achieve to prove we aren't a failure, or

- Sit back, not even trying because we are afraid of failure

In my work as a transformational coach, I see a number of high achievers stuck with this anxiety. Their drive is motivated by fear of failing. Not getting it right. To convince themselves they can, they keep pushing forward. But guess what? That fear of failure always follows a few steps behind. Waiting to pounce or undermine at any moment of hesitation, self-doubt, uncertainty. They're all seen as failure.

What an incredible level of pressure to live under. Having to check and recheck everything in the hope that we can stay a few feet ahead. This side of the 'having to get it right' coin means we can't stop – over-thinking and doing, putting too much energy into everything we do.

Meanwhile, the underachievers are stuck doing what they have always done – nothing, because hiding in the familiar keeps the fear bit at bay. Just a little. They find confidence in the familiar – they know what they are doing. But by limiting experience, underachievers also keep themselves small.

In both cases, this stuckness is all about fear of judgement. What will other people think? Especially when the fear is proven correct and we don't get it right. But in reality? It is not only about fearing the judgement of others, but also not wanting to hear the abuse of our own critical mind, our troll. We are judging ourselves. Reinforcing low self-esteem and lack of confidence. I am sure we all know how nasty and horrible our troll can be to us (until we learn self-kindness).

Either way, this negative perspective always means it will be our mistakes which stand out to us. We never give ourselves a pat on the back or a well done for trying something new, only focusing on the failure. The more we see failure, the more the strands of the sticky web wrap around us – pulling us down and undermining forward movement.

HOW TO SHIFT

In a word: kindness. Kindness to yourself. The key to personal awareness and forward movement has to begin with your relationship with yourself.

I often advise people to imagine saying all the horrible things their troll says to them to a young child. Would they be so vile? Would you? No, I'm sure you wouldn't. So why are we so vile to ourselves? Why do we beat ourselves up – expecting and fearing failure at the same time?

The truth of the matter is that what we expect, we will get. Thus reinforcing and inhibiting any forward movement. So how about giving that troll a pep talk?

Switch perspectives and focus on the half full rather than the half empty.

Each time you judge yourself for not being good enough (reinforcing fear of failure), counterbalance it with a well done for trying. Or pause a moment from fast-forward achievement to give yourself credit for where you are despite this self-destructive tendency.

Ask yourself:

- Where did this self-doubt come from?
- What does failure mean?
- Do I see others in this light? Or just admire them for trying?

Give yourself credit and encouragement to step out of what you know and learn about what you don't know. Of course, there will be errors along the way, for they are our best teachers. Step out of the stuckness and get going, not to prove you are not a failure, but for the sheer deliciousness of new adventures and skills. Become your personal cheerleader. For if you do not become your own best friend, there is a chance you will become your own worst energy.

Ruminating

I love this word. I like the sound of it. I like its meaning – chewing the cud. Makes me think of my childhood, watching the cows lying in the field next door, doing nothing. Content with just chewing. Over and over again.

Ruminating may be best left with cows or goats, as for them, it serves a purpose. Something they need to do to process their food. But it's not the same with us.

Yes, we too can sit around chewing the cud – chewing over and over the past. Reliving it. But unlike the cow, we don't find it productive. It keeps us stuck in memories which we cannot change. No matter how many conversations we have in our head about how we could have, should have done something different or how much anger we fuel by focusing on injustice, the past is past. Done and dusted. Meant to fade away into the earlier chapters in our book of life.

Caught up in overthinking, we are like a needle on a record, stuck in the same groove. We are not letting the past go. Which is an effective way to strengthen stuckness. Why? Because we are totally occupied, and while we're caught up in what's gone before, what lies ahead is not even on the drawing board.

Ruminating is like a puzzle we can't do. Not all the pieces are in the box. It can never be finished. What happened in the past has happened. We cannot change it. No matter how many conversations we replay or how much pain we revisit, the past has passed. It's done.

When this thread of the stuckness web pulls us into the past, it keeps us there. Which means our attention is not in the present, nor looking to the future. We're living in our heads. Living in the past. And unlike my neighbour the cow chewing on what she has already eaten, we serve no purpose by ruminating on the past other than causing emotional pain.

While we should be driving forward, this stuckness drives us backwards. Sitting with our back to the road ahead, we are not engaged. Unable to see the way forward because our focus only sees where we've been. But just like we cannot finish the useless incomplete puzzle, we cannot travel backwards. Why? Because the car of time comes without reverse.

HOW TO SHIFT

On some level, we need to accept what has happened. Whatever, however, whoever, reliving the past, overthinking, only fuels pain and stops healing. Like an open wound, the more we keep hitting it, the less likely it will heal. It is the same with emotional pain.

The act of chewing the cud for us humans serves no purpose, but learning from the past does. As with all things, there is negative and positive, and when we stop the negative of trying to change the past, we can then access the positive. Learning from the situation means we mitigate the risk of repeating the pattern. But even if we choose to let it go completely and not look for greater understanding, this very act – accepting what has happened – releases the stuckness thread. Energy flows, which feels a heck of a lot better than the chew, chew, chew.

Ask yourself:

- How does my chewing the cud serve me? How does it hinder me?
- What is so hard to let go of?
- Do I need to forgive myself or others to regain my peace of mind?

Sometimes we have to lose to win. In the very act of letting something from our past go, we are gaining so much more of ourselves. There is a lot of wisdom in the accepting of what is or, in this case, what was.

Super-judgemental

Within all of us is the critical voice. When it's positive, it's constructive. Helping us learn from mistakes, review and change behaviour accordingly. In other words, it encourages personal growth.

But what if we aren't growing? What if we drink from the half-empty side of the glass? Stuck in the same place – same mindset?

Remember stuckness doesn't feel so good, and unhappiness fuels judgement. When we focus on lack, feeding anxiety and negativity, this powerful critical inner voice becomes our troll – a battering ram with which to beat ourselves. That's the pattern. It is through negative thinking we give power to self-negation and judgement.

This sadly keeps us in a holding pattern that's darn uncomfortable. Becoming fearful of the judgement of others (fearful that they will see we are not good enough), we can jump into judging them first. Finding fault with them overlays them finding fault with us. A form of self-defence. But one which is pure illusion. For these sticky strands of stuckness form glasses of unkindness which notice only ignorance and uselessness.

Like all things, this has a positive. For while we are busy judging others, we deflect from our feeling of inability, our lack of self-belief. For a moment, we move attention from ourselves. The voice of the self-judgemental troll, negative and critical, is otherwise occupied.

A rather cruel stuckness this one (whether to ourselves or others) as there is no resolution, no change. We're stuck wearing glasses which are far from rose tinted. And if we see a need for change? Always it is the need for change in others.

HOW TO SHIFT

We have to lose the glasses. For they empower stuckness. As long as we remain eager to find fault, either within or without, we will never find the solution to forward movement. There is a core belief which needs shifting – the one where we believe we aren't good enough, worthy. This will never give us the chance to change.

But what's the truth of the matter?

Every single person is a result of conditioning and past experiences. And yes, like us, sometimes others feel they're not good enough. Frightened of what other people think. But that is just a pebble in the path of life. It is not the path itself.

When we step on the path of personal growth and awareness, we open up to who we are now and learn to refine. Let go of outdated conditionings which do not suit us. Probably never did. Yet we believed what we were told to believe. We were a disappointment. A mess-up. Not smart enough (and the list goes on).

There's not simply the worthy and the unworthy, but levels of awareness which teach refinement, self-love and kindness. As I sit here now (perhaps not in a good place), I can easily block my writing. How? I judge my words. With clouded glasses, I see only what is wrong. Not good enough. Which can easily reinforce the fear that I don't have a clue what I am on about, and why did I ever think I did? In other words, judging creates stuckness.

To lose the glasses, we need to learn to see ourselves differently. No longer through the eyes of negative conditioning. We have to stop being so darn cruel. Make friends with ourselves. Let go of judgement. Step into forgiveness. For when we do, the stuckness webs begins to loosen. We learn to love ourselves – warts and all.

Ask yourself:

- How much easier would life be if I focused on supportive self-dialogue rather than keep giving myself a hard time?
- Where would that take me?
- Where would I like to go?

Fuelling the dream, not the fear, make yourself a promise to encourage positive change and notice how quickly those pebbles of self-discomfort are left behind. Oh yeah – and get yourself some new glasses. Ones which see you, and everyone else, in a better light.

Increased frustration

We are energy, and if energy doesn't connect with the world in a positive, productive and creative way – sharing our unique self – it will thrash about inside. Think of a dog who seldom gets a really good run outside. He's stuck in the house all day. All the energy that desperately needs expressing and loves to run builds up. What do we get? An unhappy, uncomfortable, irritable four-legged creature. And we humans are not any different.

We all have gifts to share, and our unique self doesn't like it when it's excused away or ignored. This stuckness pattern is extremely uncomfortable. Trapped energy always is. When we're frustrated, we're not suffering from lack of energy, but from excess energy which has no outlet. Like all avenues to stuckness, it colours our life. But not brightly. Unused energy builds pressure which, not surprisingly, is so uncomfortable it will come out biting.

HOW TO SHIFT

The image that always comes to my mind with this stuckness is of a medieval tower. Drawbridge up. Moat surrounding it. But this one also has a second level of defence – a row of guards standing to attention.

Why all the protection? The level of frustration inside the tower is so great, wouldn't it make sense to lower the drawbridge, do away with the guards and gallop off into the sunset?

The bridge is up, the guards on duty for a good reason. When frustrated, we are buying into the tower. Whether because we believe we can't leave – perhaps those guards aren't ours but employed to keep us where we are – or because no matter how uncomfortable, it feels safe.

As with all states of stuckness, the tower has a positive as well as a negative energy held within. Towers offer protection. Keeping us safe and defending us. But from what?

Change. Taking a chance. Doing something different.

Frustrated energy is powerful. The power bouncing about inside can feel overwhelming. Overwhelming what? Us. So we are protecting ourselves from our own energy. The capability of self. Which – let's face it – can be daunting. We are that amazing. And that's the irony.

Here we are, investing a lot to keeping energy in. Why? What's the fear? What would happen if it was released? What would we do with it? Too many changes would have to happen. Too much responsibility. So we batten down the hatches and live uncomfortably.

To shift this state, we need to take responsibility for our energy outside the tower. The ability to respond. Step up a gear.

The good news is energy will flow where it is directed. Keep changes manageable, but allow yourself to do what you want to do. Even if it means creating a totally radical lifestyle. For within the energy of desire is the ability to create.

Acknowledging the need to let down the drawbridge is not only an outlet for expansion, but also an open door. Which works both ways, allowing energy to flow in as well as out. Rest assured, change will reveal itself, and with it will come the lovely feeling of discovery.

Ask yourself

· What have I always wanted to do, but feel I can't, it's too late or I'm too afraid?

Now imagine yourself doing just that. Get used to the idea that to lose your stuckness, you have to lower the drawbridge. And the tower? You can leave it there, and if it feels like you need to scurry back for a while, that's OK too. You don't have to be perfect. Just open to learning.

Advising others, but not yourself

Let's face it, we're all full of good advice, some more than others. And we're happy to offer it, because hey! Who doesn't want to help a friend in need? It is a natural way to reach out. To support. Also, it's a win-win situation as we both feel better for it. Nothing like helping solve another's dilemma, or at least advising them on the best course of action to take.

In the weird way of life, it seems so easy to see what someone else should do. Their problems are much more visible compared to ours. And certainly, they're easier to solve as we tell them what to do and they do the doing.

If we would just listen to our free advice, we would learn so much about our needs. For there are never any wasted words. All have power and give insight. These strands of the stuckness web are coated with a feel-good action. Helping and advising is a ride on the wave of connection. That wonderful energy which flows through one to the other. So not only are we wise, we're also helping someone to change. Good strategy. We get to feel good while pushing someone else's change button.

Now I'm not saying that's a bad thing. Of course not. If we can't help one another, what is the point? But while we are good at giving, are we also good at taking?

When advice is only allowed to travel on a one-way road, from us to others, we are blocking help and support being extended our way. Just as we can see them, they can see us. But we can be invisible to ourselves, making it tough to change.

This strand keeps us stuck because innately, we all know what the next step should be. But maybe, just maybe, we don't want to listen.

Energy attracts similar energy. Often our words pouring forth are the same words we need to hear or reconnect with. Listening is a way for inner wisdom to get through. And wisdom works in all directions. But sometimes we have the capability to be as thick as planks. Usually when change is involved.

HOW TO SHIFT

Be more aware of the hold this stuckness has on you. If you go around full of good advice when no one is asking for it, then there is a bit of an imbalance. A good thing to keep in mind is that, just like you, sometimes others don't want or are not ready to hear your advice. They may have things to work out first. But if you keep giving, taking up the airspace and not listening, guess what? Your advice will go unheard.

The best way to restore the balance of giving and receiving advice is to be mindful and really listen to what you say to others. Take your own advice. Not only from you to them, or them to you, but also your inner words of wisdom and encouragement.

Ask yourself:

- Honestly – am I really good at giving free advice or do I like the feeling of giving it?
- Do I listen to others?
- Do I listen to myself?

As with all of life, balance is key. Please don't stop being helpful, but listen first. The other person just may have it all sorted. Change already underway. Encourage their wisdom to take action. Then turn some of that unique knowing back on yourself and you too will become visible, as will the next steps to take.

Words have power. Listen well.

Negative thinking

While positivity opens us up to opportunity and growth, and promotes change, negativity shuts the door. Believing in the half-empty glass, we focus on lack. It is fear-based thinking.

I remember having a chat with someone who took pride in being negative (each to their own). I was curious as to the positive of being negative. Their argument, said with great pride, 'When faced with a situation, I always think of the worst that can happen. Then when it doesn't, I am pleasantly surprised.'

Granted, I can see the logic. If we know the worst that could happen, we will know what we need to do if it does happen. A survival plan. But what about the feeling? Not the logic.

While imagining all the outcome disasters, we are also feeling them. Fuelling negativity. Which stomps out the wonderful energy of possibility, hope, belief.

OK, say the pair of us hear that new neighbours will be moving in. Until it actually happens, depending on how we think, we are fuelling feelings. Personally, I would much rather keep my peace of mind and believe that our neighbours will be quiet, friendly and accommodating, perhaps becoming new friends, than walk around fuelling the feeling of upcoming disaster by believing they will be inconsiderate, rude or downright nasty.

If the negative thinker turns out to be right, for a brief moment, they feel justified. They knew the new neighbours were going to be a horror show. But at what expense? How long have they made themselves miserable every time they imagined these horrible neighbours? I, on the other hand, am still positive. Disappointed too, but I'll soon pick myself up and look for a positive path forward with a challenging situation.

And if they are lovely? The negative thinker can feel good about the fact their worst-case fears haven't been realised. But again, how long have they felt horrible, supporting fear with negativity?

This stuckness strand thinks away change. Fearing it. Looking for the worst that can happen so it makes sense not to take a chance. But does it make sense?

How we think affects everything about us. Including health. When negative, we expect disappointment. Seeing only lack, we fuel our perspective with fear. Perspective is the key word here – how we look at life is how we experience life.

When we are negative, we have locked ourselves down into a narrow way of thinking. Pulling negative situations from the past to support a negative view of the future, we shut out light, believing in a dark, unfriendly world. And that's the problem. We need the light – the energy of positivity – to help us make better sense of what is.

HOW TO SHIFT

The problem with trying to shift thinking from negative to positive is our thoughts, like everything else, are just part of a bigger pattern, and therefore hard to see. Often, we don't even know we are being negative. To shed this thread, we have to first become more aware of our negativity.

An effective way to cast light on how you think is with the positive affirmation. Say, 'I am Positive' 200 times a day – you don't have to count, just keep repeating 'I am Positive. I am Positive.' Imagine each affirmation like a ray of light, shining down into an overgrown, dark swamp (your subconscious). This won't suddenly shift you into positivity, but it will help you see your negativity. Light, not darkness, helps you better see when you are negative and encourages you to reframe with a positive slant.

Ask yourself:

- Do I feel safer believing in disappointment, so if it doesn't happen, I am pleasantly surprised?
- How does being negative curtail my life and relationships?
- Are positive people not being real?

The simple truth is life is all about how we see it – perspective colours experiences. While believing the glass is half empty, we focus on emptiness. When the glass is half full? We always know there is enough.

Apathy

In this state, we do not care about stuckness. Long since having given up on the idea of forward movement, we have disengaged. Allowing strands to form a web around us. With no movement, dust collects on the cobweb of neglect. Trapped by lack of interest, we have neither enthusiasm nor concern. We're not at all bothered. Not only about what is going on around us, but within as well. We just don't care.

Tricky one, this. To shake off the dust, break free from the dulled sticky stuckness web, we need to care. But how can we care if we don't care? It is a resignation of Spirit. Easier perhaps to deal with, for when we don't care, we don't feel.

What's interesting is that the German origin of the word care is *chara*: wail, lament. Perhaps that is why there is a disengagement – we're not wanting to feel the powerful emotion of grief.

But the prisoner of this web was not always like this. In fact, I would say they probably cared too much. So much it hurt. So to stop the pain, they opted out. Sitting now in the back corner of themselves, they're not bothered. Or more to the point, they're not letting themselves be bothered, because when they do let the power of feelings through, a tidal wave sweeps in.

The web? The apathy? This is a protection, a belief it is far better not to be involved than to feel powerless in a world which just doesn't feel enough.

But it takes a lot of energy to stay stuck. Combine this with shutting off the feeling tap, and the pressure builds. There is a safeguard in this pattern as every so often, the dam bursts, allowing movement. But with this problem of caring while not wanting to, when the pressure builds and the dam breaks, the energy that moves is usually defensive. Anger. A hard edge protecting the soft Heart. Once out, the pressure drops and the sticky web is reinforced. Its wearer then moves back into a small corner of themselves.

HOW TO SHIFT

It doesn't have to be this way.

You feel so much because you are a powerful person. The power of you lies in your Heart. Combined with great sensitivity, the injustice of the world can overload you.

We grieve for many things: people, situations, lost dreams, missing time. But like all emotions, grief is there for a reason. It has its part to play, and if we pull out of the process before the natural ebb and flow of loss has had a chance to subside, we will keep the grief alive. We'll always be afraid of the power, of its surges.

The world needs more sensitive, feeling people. The same strength you use to keep your detachment – keep yourself stuck – could be used to help so many connect deep inside themselves. And who better to help another see the value of feelings than one who has the ability to take that deep dive?

Feelings are our barometer. They clue us in and connect us to each other. That web you are so wrapped up in? It's not really protecting you, but keeping you further away from yourself. Like with any stuckness, to get moving, you first need to see where you are and be open to finding a different way of being. In this instance, allow your Heart to feel.

Ask yourself:

- Have I always been this way?
- When did I decide to detach? What hurt way too much?

- Would it help to talk with someone to help heal the grief?
- What is the worst that could happen? When I'm not caring, is there a big part of me grieving for myself?

Caring is an aspect of loving. When we wriggle free from the web of neglect, the Heart resumes a rhythm which is individual and true to ourselves. When we connect into our truth, there is no way that we can't care. Why? Because we have always wanted to. And doing what is natural is really something to care about.

Fear of change

Not to state the obvious, but change changes things. And that could be the problem.

When tied up in this sticky strand, we hold ourselves back from making any changes. Why? Because there is no certainty with the unknown. Not only do we not know how something will work out, we also have no certainty it *will* work out. Who's to say that change won't make life worse than it is?

We are born with two innate fears: fear of falling and fear of loud noises. Any other fear is learned. If we have a fear of change, the change itself would have to have been the teacher.

Often those with this stuckness strand have a painful history of huge changes being thrust upon them. One of those changes, where suddenly the rug was pulled out from underneath them, caused all they thought they knew to spin out of control as they tumbled downwards. It's understandable, then, that they would fear change. If that was how I defined change – as huge, tumultuous experiences – I too would be nervous when it came knocking at my door.

When we have a fear of change, it is easy to rationalise away any forward movement. By sticking with what we know, we remain in our comfort zone. We know where we are. We are in the familiar with a level of security. Our energy takes the easiest route. One in which we don't have to think.

But everything in life must change. Just watch nature change season to season so every living thing can grow. And so must we. That's the thing about change. We are changing all the time (just look in the mirror). It is natural. We cannot stop it happening, just as the tree cannot hang on to the apple just because it may be afraid to lose its fruit. Change happens. It is a process of transformation. When we ignore or push change away, we are going against nature. And nature has a way of balancing energy.

I am reminded of the story of a woman renting a neglected house. She keeps telling herself she's got to move. Everything is breaking down around her, but she ignores the need to find a new home. Then one day, the roof falls in. She has to move. Make the change she knew she needed to make all along. But now she doesn't have the luxury of time.

When we hold back the tide of time, change tends to create havoc. Why? It is only catching up on back-dated changes we needed to make. Fearing, ignoring, refusing to embrace necessary change makes life more difficult.

Change does not have to be big. When we fear change, we only see it in extra-large. No. Change comes in many sizes and shapes. We can change our socks and feel good.

HOW TO SHIFT

To shift this stuckness, the fear of change, first learn to redefine the size of the fear. Make change manageable. Choose what you want to change, and then make it reasonable. Little steps will still get you up the mountain.

Start small. Focus on your environment. Something you feel comfortable with. For example, could you paint a room a different colour? Get used to the energy that change brings. Usually one change sets off a train of them. A new colour scheme in the bedroom, maybe new furniture, prompts a good clean out. See how it goes?

By building your confidence with change, you lessen the fear. The wounds of the past slip back into the past.

Then without you even knowing, change just starts to happen, as indeed it was meant to do.

Ask yourself:

- What happened which stopped me in my tracks?
- Do I want to live with this fear, knowing I can't stop change anyway?
- What little change can I make today to better acquaint myself with its wonderful transformative energy?

Yes, change changes things. But then, how natural is it to keep everything the same? How impossible? Fears holds us back. This one serves no purpose except to keep stuckness alive. The tree we met earlier? It relaxes, knowing it's OK to let go of the apple, because that process ensures more will follow.

Analysis paralysis

We have an amazing capacity to think. To work things out, view them from all angles. Weighing, measuring, checking and double-checking information. Mulling over the input of others. Judging from past experiences. Quelling the fear of any potential results we need to confirm and reaffirm. Check, recheck.

Herein lies the danger: overthinking.

Imagine the mind like the world wide web. Information overload. Need to know how to do something? Ask Siri. Check out YouTube. Search the web. There's bound to be a number of different takes on whatever information you need to help make that decision.

Now imagine that you have all this information, all different perspectives, different layers of what you seek, but, hmm... there is still a part of you that doesn't quite trust it. Not so sure, you delve further and further into the web. Spending more and more time gathering, reviewing, analysing, until like Alice, you have fallen so far down the rabbit hole, it seems there is no way up. Overloaded with too many variables, your initial action plan now seems far away.

No longer trusting in what you know, you have to keep looking. Thinking. Thinking. Thinking. Covering every eventuality, every unknown. Which is quite tricky, as an unknown is exactly that.

Simply put, the analysis paralysis strand ties you up in knots. Overthinking kills desire. Whatever you'd set out to do – buy a new car, change jobs – is stamped out. The decision is now far too hard.

We can all have too much of a good thing. In this case? Too much information.

HOW TO SHIFT

Why do we feel we always need more information? Wrapped in the sticky distrust of self, we seek more knowledge to help quell the fear of uncertainty. That uncertainty lies within. Decisions move energy forward. But when we're caught in the loop of indecision, all we do is go around and around until the overload stops us totally. Analysis paralysis.

The good news? There is more to us than our ability to think. We also have the ability to feel. Gut reaction. It doesn't matter how much information we gather or how many variables we cover, if something feels right, it generally is. The rest of it is just knotted stuckness.

To release this strand, step out of the pattern of overthinking. Become more aware of the 'Yes, do it!' or 'No, not a good idea' gut reactions. Feelings are barometers, telling us about the winds of change. By taking the chance of trusting yourself, you'll grow your confidence. Forward movement will happen. Suddenly, your life will reflect the growth and vitality which change offers. And the more you trust your inner wisdom, the easier it is to hear.

Ask yourself:

- When I'm faced with a decision, what is the worst that can happen? And if it does, what will I do?
- More importantly, what will I miss out on if I don't take that chance?

Then ask, is this the right action to take? Listen well. Your gut will tell you – either a lovely, warm feeling or a warning. Either way, no doubt later on you will realise how much your gut just knows what to do. Your job? Listen. Listen well and learn to trust.

Fearing life has passed you by

For many of us, this is a fairly common stuckness strand, and it easily pulls us down. Why? Because it is fuelled by fear of ageing. When we suddenly (as that is how it seems) have more time behind us than we expect to have in front of us, a bit of panic sets in. It's almost as though our life force is doing the stirring. Making us uncomfortable. Reminding us we are living on a deadline.

Then the judgemental troll comes out to play. Looking at all the opportunities we never grasped, the dreams we've yet to fulfil, the challenges we stepped away from. The weakness we never strengthened. And now what? We're too old. It's too late.

But is it?

For as long we inhale and exhale, we are alive. Which means life has not passed us by, but is walking hand in hand with us. Believing it's too late, we're too old, fuels resignation. Negativity and fear turn up their volume, drowning out any possibilities of grabbing life by the tail. Then we berate ourselves. Which is a bit cruel.

When we step into the fear of life passing us by, where does that leave us? Feeling bad about the life we've led? But, hello? It's not over. We're still breathing.

As we become what we think, failure is all we see. We believe we should have got it together. Could have done this or that. But thanks to our negative perspective, the boat has left the port. Without us. Looking around at the empty dock, we judge ourselves, fuelling resignation. Accepting defeat.

Why? Remember stuckness is strengthened by fear. We believe it, so it is. With more time behind than before us, we are immobilised. Not trying to turn the tide. Living on a low ebb. Believing it's too late. So why bother trying? Downward slope from here on as we tumble into later life, disappointed with ourselves, our choices and actions not taken.

HOW TO SHIFT

As always, perspective is key. If you believe it is too late, then yes, it is. For your belief will have it no other way. But to shed this fear of missing the boat, you need to recognise that, just as in nature, everything has a time to bloom. So be a late bloomer. Show the world how to live until you die, not just wait until you die.

I have started a little collection of YouTube videos of amazing elders of this world who are not letting age stop them. If anything, they are using the deadline (great motivators, deadlines) to do what they always wanted to do. For example, the man who, at seventy-five, decided he had done his bit with his family and now it was about him. Doing what he'd always wanted to do, he started ballet lessons. He's now eighty and spends most days practising in the dance studio. With more energy and vitality than ever before, he engages fully with life.

Ask yourself:

- Without any judgement, what would I love to do, see, be, experience?
- Isn't it time I stopped stopping myself and started starting myself?
- How good would I feel if I did this? How much more alive?

Shift your perspective. See what others are doing because they have not allowed age to be a factor. By not saying no to life, they are saying yes to experience. Fuelling life force and Spirit. What's to lose? Only your fear. Use it as a motivation.

The funny thing about fear – the more power you give it, the less you have yourself. Take back your power and plough it into your world of new experiences. Creating flexibly of the mind and Spirit shakes away the limitations of stuckness.

Lost in thought – getting unstuck

- Take away the power from the negative. Choose to find the positive.

- Embrace the unknown. Confidence builds by doing.

- Communicate – get social. It's all too easy to drown in thought. Talking with others changes focus and creates balance.

- Volunteer – do a good deed. Supporting another person brings you into action and opens the Heart.

- Leap – what's the worst that can happen? What's the best? Knowing the answer helps shift perspective.

- Practise mindfulness. By shifting focus to being present in the world, you find beauty.

- Accept fear – reframe it. Fear and excitement are similar sensations. Choose to be excited.

- Fuelling positive reassurance strengthens a positive mindset.

- Make little changes – get used to changing. After all, change is natural. Just look out your window. Nature is always changing.

- Chunk it down. Take manageable steps. Little steps will still lead to the top of the mountain.

- Let it go. Leaving the past in the past means it settles into an earlier life story. No longer feeding the pain, it lies forgotten unless you choose to learn from that experience.

- Be kind to yourself (and to others). We all need to support self-love.

- Get physical, taking you out of your mind and into your body.

- Get inspired – if someone else can do it, you can too.

FIVE

Up In The Air

I recall my mom being surprised at my intelligence. For most of my life, she had seen me as the pretty one who lived in another world. It is not unusual for sensitive, intuitive, artistic people to be viewed this way. Bit airy fairy. Spiritually inclined, highly imaginative and creative, flitting from one idea to the other with few reaching fruition. In other words, living up in the air.

I also remember the day that all changed.

I was in my early thirties, a long way into self-discovery and personal growth. Walking down the street, not really thinking about anything, just enjoying the summer's day, I suddenly had a weirdly palpable sensation of a tail growing out from my coccyx and into the earth behind me. As I walked, it trailed behind.

I was soon to realise that this was a momentous occasion in my life. Extraordinarily life-changing. But at that time, my overall feeling was that I felt huge and cumbersome. Like I had the biggest bum on Earth – swinging from side to side with each step I took.

That was the day I connected with gravity. The day I dropped down from living above myself and firmly planted my feet on the ground. My life shifted from potentiality into practicality. I was more present in the world around me with gravity as my rudder.

It is not surprising that of three mindsets, it is this one that contains a few key stucknesses that I can really relate to.

Needless to say, living above ourselves, up in the air, feels like darn hard work. Lack of attention span, poor memory, too sensitive, no drive, not able to get from here to there, although we always can see the potential. It has a lot to answer for.

Whether we're floating above ourselves or tucked away deep inside our tower of protection (I use 'up in the air' as a cover-all term here), there is a disconnect between our Spirit and ourselves and, inevitably, the world around us. This is not an uncommon phenomenon. Many of my clients are living life like they exist in a hot-air balloon without the ability to land.

But we all need a grounding rod. When we float above, we seek people who are solid and practical, throw our rope down and latch on to their energy. Their life, so much easier to see than ours (after all, we are looking down from above), can soon become more important than our own. A great way for stuckness to set the strands in concrete around us.

But the Earth affords us a life-giving energy as well, and when we disconnect for whatever reason, we lose out on the strength it offers. The choice is either live in fantasy or despair. Remember, if we disconnect, we can't get from here (our idea) to there (our goal). Energy is not directed.

There are many reasons for disconnecting. Born sensitive, I took years to get my feet on the ground. But trauma, fear, illness can loosen our footing as well.

When we are up in the air, one of the most frustrating challenges is our lack of follow through, whether it's because of low self-esteem, believing we can't achieve what we set out to do, or the practical lack of Earth energy, which is unavailable to us. Like any stuckness mindset, it's hugely frustrating.

Have a read through the ten up-in-the-air stucknesses. You may see yourself in one or gain understanding of another. I don't want you to feel you have to have an earth-shattering tail-growing experience as I did or you will always remain slightly disconnected from yourself, up in the air. Personal awareness has a lot to offer, and I have witnessed many clients either touching down for the first time or reconnecting with the Earth. And when they do? Stuckness drops away and their life starts moving forward.

One of the key components to change is seeing where you are. And – of course – without judgement.

Boredom

As a child, I remember complaining to my mom, 'I'm bored. What should I do?' Her inevitable response?

'Take off your hat and spit in your shoe.'

I had no idea what that meant, but it worked every time as a mental interrupter. While I was trying to figure it out, the boredom left the station. Forgotten. Then I went away and found something to do.

That's the key.

Boredom means lack of change. Without change, life stays the same – we're doing what we've always done. Our energy pattern becomes repetitive, flatlines, often leading to a dull, uninterested mind. Our life has fallen asleep, suffering from lack of stimuli. There's nothing new (no struggles or challenges) as time passes. This stuckness strand wraps around our eyes, blinding us to the possibility that we can shift this state while robbing us of the need for a mental interrupter – the value of change.

HOW TO SHIFT

The energy of this stuckness state is stagnancy. Nothing moving. Therein lies the solution – movement. Yes. Even if you can't be bothered.

The challenge with this thread is the blindfold. Part of you is happy with boredom. It is not a particularly uncomfortable energy pattern. You are not in pain. You are not putting on weight (ie it doesn't show). But with this pattern, your energy has congealed. Not going anywhere, you are bored by this stuckness.

So that is a good thing?

Through the act of saying, 'I am bored', you bring the stuckness state into light. It is far easier to change something you see than that which lies hidden. Also, through the acknowledgement, you express that you want it gone. Like me going to my mom, asking her what I could do. I wanted to be free of the boredom. I wanted to be engaged. Interested.

Movement is key.

The tendency is to sit in congealed energy. Wanting it to change, but not doing anything. But you have to move. Get up and get going. Movement then attracts more movement. Even washing the dishes that have been left far too long gives you a sense of completion. The energy of completion naturally prompts a new beginning.

Boredom, once acknowledged, is begging you to change. That may seem a step too far, but like any journey, the act of putting one foot in front of the other gets the shift shifting.

First make a change in your environment. One that needs doing. The need will get the ball rolling. Then step back and focus on the difference you've created. Order is a great reminder of capability, which is a sight more comfortable than boredom.

One of the ways I shift out of the boredom web is to go into my office and organise my filing cabinet. A great mental interrupter as with each paper or file I handle, my mind is stimulated.

Change the state – change the feeling.

Ask yourself:

- Do I want to stay bored?
- What in my immediate environment needs doing?

Then go and do it – complete the task. Step away and get that good feeling of finishing. Then use that energy to move to the next thing. Little steps create forward momentum, leaving behind congealment and stepping in the stirrings of flow.

Lack of vitality

I am sure that most of us have experienced not having enough oomph! Feeling exhausted, too tired.

Everything we need to do seems to be a huge effort, and depending on the reason for this lack of vitality, we may feel the effort to do it requires more energy than we have.

Years ago, when I was recovering from viral meningitis, my battery was so depleted that the thought of doing anything at all seemed way out of the ballpark. And when I absolutely had to do something? I would imagine throwing out a hook with a rope attached to it. It would hook on to my destination, and then I would imagine myself pulling myself to get where I needed to go. Tough time. But it is a tough time when our batteries are low for whatever reason. When we're too tired or not well enough, our vitality suffers. The spark that gets us going has huge trouble catching light.

Not having much energy is a clear indicator that this stuckness strand is wrapped around us. It is not actually that we don't have enough energy, it is more that our energy is blocked in some way. Think of a river running downhill. When it reaches a dam, the water is walled, blocked. Now regulated, the river below no longer reflects the power and surge of the river upstream. The river still has water, but its power is lessened.

Lack of energy results in loss of vitality. No matter how it manifests – lowness of mood, ill health, mental fog, weakness of body or Spirit, lack of will – dammed energy stops the heathy flow found further up the mountain. This makes everything a huge effort.

When energy is blocked in whatever way, we live on a low ebb. Life is more difficult. But the good news is that energy cannot be created or destroyed (there is always the same amount of energy), so we all have enough to loosen the stranglehold of this stuckness. The challenge is finding new avenues for more water to flow. Movement follows. Vitality increases.

HOW TO SHIFT

Think of a flat battery in your car. How are you going to get it going again? The battery needs charging. Where? From another battery or power source.

When you suffer from a low ebb, you need to source other batteries you can draw benefit from. Help the recharge. To know who or what to plug in to, be more aware of what you need. Blocked energy may not give you the answer, but being open to new ideas and support will tap into the fuel of inspiration and hope. Never underestimate their power. For they are the batteries of Spirit.

When we're uplifted, we feel better. The kind word of another, an offer of help, a new avenue for healing, the comfort of a loved one – battery to battery, it is the connection which transfers the charge. When our river is running on low, by tapping into the flow of another, we can bridge separateness. Once we're connected? Energy flows. Vitality picks up.

Ask yourself:

- Is there something I can do or need to find to get the recharge I so desperately need?
- How much of my stuckness is me holding myself back? Do I push help away?
- Is there anything that I can do, manageable with the energy level I have, which will give me a boost?
- Do I need to ask for help?

Acknowledging lack of energy is not a judgement. If anything, it encourages compassion, especially for anyone who is suffering because of physical illness. But it prompts us to have a rethink – be honest with what we need and ask for help. Like when we drill a hole in the dam, energy will burst through.

Feeling like an outsider

When we feel like an outsider, we feel separate. As though life is a play and we are just the audience. Life's happening, but for everyone else. Our thinking is either clouded or fuelled by anxiety. Memory suffers, as does vitality.

Low energy levels and lack of focus make it incredibly hard to get on and do. With everything feeling like a huge effort, it's easier to pull back. Just watch the play.

What is going on?

In contrast, imagine your body is a container which holds the essence of you. Filling out every bit of the physical container, you are present in you. Which is not only a solid feeling, but also one of great power. With better focus and clarity, you then become present in the world. There is a feeling of empowerment. Why? Because energy (remember, you are a ball of energy) works best when contained. Think of water. It's far easier to drink it from a glass rather than lap at a puddle.

When feeling like outsiders, we have a lack of presence. We have pretty much left the body. There is some of us left (otherwise we would have reached our deadline), but there's more floating around in the space above us. Like smoke, it goes wherever it's blown, but has no control of its own. We feel we have no active part in life. Absent from what's around us, we hang out on the ceiling or watching from the sidelines.

This sticky strand keeps us hanging by a thread, so lacks strength and vitality, as well as connection. Because it is so hard to see ourselves when we are not behind our eyes, but floating in the space above. Float, forget, float some more.

There are lots of reasons why we find ourselves on the periphery of life, shock being a major one. The challenge with this stuckness is in the re-knitting. To see we are stuck, we need to see the thread, strengthen our connection to it, and then once we've settled back inside ourselves, cut it away.

HOW TO SHIFT

What is lacking with this stuckness is an Earth connection. Remember, disconnected energy floats above you. So the key to helping you release this pattern is tapping into the Earth's energy, which acts as a magnet, bringing your back to yourself.

This explains why so many find going for a walk in the country or working in the garden valuable. The Earth's energy vibrates slower than ours, pulling us down out of our heads. There is a reason why a plug's wiring needs that all-important Earth connection. The grounding makes it safe. We also need grounding. A strong need to feel safe.

In my work as a transformational coach, I see a great number of people living on the outside of their lives. It is not uncommon. Some are more disconnected than others, but when I help them shift back into themselves, they all experience great change. They feel like they've reconnected with an old friend. Like they've been missing themselves and never even knew it. Not only happier, the mind more comfortable, they also strangely say they feel taller. The container has been filled. With the stuckness energy released, they are able to participate in life and move forward.

We all feel better when we're engaged with life.

Ask yourself:

- Am I fuzzy headed? Spacey? Lacking energy, yet have way too much zooming about in my head?
- Why is everything such a huge effort?

- Have I always been like this?

With all stuckness strands, you have to see them to shift them. But with this one, you don't feel safe on a deep level. You'll have disconnected for a reason.

Go out into nature. Be aware of a shift, no matter how subtle. Begin the process of earthing – grounding. Get back on that stage, taking up the role of who you are meant to be.

Lack of joy

As we know, energy needs to move, to flow, and becomes darn uncomfortable when it doesn't. With lack of energy, we run on empty. Which, if you think about it, is quite a difficult thing to do.

When everything is an effort, life seems like hard work, so intolerable we narrow down. Feeling low, we eventually settle for lowness. Thinking atrophies. We lock ourselves away.

Think about a riverbed dried out by drought. Thirsty animals fight one another to draw from the damp left behind. Life is hard. When we lack joy, we feel a similar deprivation. Believing there is not enough energy to go around, that our thirst will never be quenched. Everything is too much of a struggle, and for what? The energy of lack of joy is like a neglected window, needing a good wash. Any sunlight is dulled, fighting to get through the filthy glass. Which means the house we've holed ourselves up in cannot benefit from its rays. We are disconnected from the world around us.

Joy is like one of those rays of sunlight. Not only does it reach out, giving vitality and warmth, it also illuminates. We can see more of what is. In contrast, when we just accept our lot and never change anything, we allow the dust of neglect to take hold, pulling us down into a low ebb of life.

The very purpose of the energy of joy is to uplift. But what if it can't get through our tough exterior because we have long since stopped believing? Separated from this light-enhancing energy of laughter, connectedness, love, we will atrophy. Eventually shutting down as negativity drags us into a small corner of who we are. It is not that there is no joy. There is always joy – nature constantly fuels joy – it just depends on how we think. If we refuse to look, it will go unnoticed. Unfelt.

Remember this stuckness has an investment in keeping everything the same. The positive is it offers control, especially when we feel we don't have any. Safe inside our tower, we know where we are. Know how to manage. And although joy fuels the battery of life, just as sunlight breaking through a clouded sky lifts our spirits, when our battery is low, we believe it's not worth the bother of trying. We can't get from here to there. Sadly, even when we're offered help in the form of hope, our negative thinking rules it out as possible.

HOW TO SHIFT

Lack of joy is unnatural. It is a state of resignation. Of disappointment, pain and struggle. Isolated, we run into the tower of neglect.

First things first. Recognise that we all need one another. It is your thinking forming the walls around you and neglect which leaves the windows unwashed.

The energy of joy is light shining from one Heart to another. So you have to start to feel. Be open to feeling. There is always a reason behind our shutting down, but see it as a transient state and be open to moving through it. A Spirit calling for help will never go unnoticed.

Joy gives us the giggles. Uplifting, it recharges and enhances our energy for life. Maybe just the recognition that you have shut yourself away will be enough to prompt you to get out the rags and start cleaning those windows. Realisation is a powerful force for movement.

Ask yourself:

- When did I shut down?
- How is that serving me?
- What action can I take to allow others to connect to me?

Joy heals. It is contagious. You just need to be open to catching the virus of sharing.

Creatively blocked

Creative people talk about being in the flow. A wonderful feeling where the book writes itself, the painting takes form automatically, the choir harmonises. All that is needed from the creative is to be there to tap the keys, put paint on the brush, raise their voice in song. The rest feels like a wonderful dance. Not concerned about leading, we can just enjoy the movement, its grace.

Creative energy has its own flow that's both delicious and awe inspiring. When we surf the wave of creative flow, we are one with the process. Right there with it. In the moment.

But what about if the dance suddenly stops? The wave falls away?

Imagine two fields side by side, separated by a fence. One is the feeling field, the other the thinking field. When our creative energy is flowing, we are hanging out in the feeling field. The process feels amazing, effortless.

But when that lovely process becomes a struggle, we have stepped out of the flow. We have jumped over the stile and are now looking at our project from afar. As we're no longer in the feeling field, in steps the critical mind.

That's the block.

No longer riding the wave of what feels right, we are looking and judging what's not right. As the critical mind searches for fault, the creative energy flow loses momentum. Remember that stuckness strand? It's now wrapping around our feet. The longer we stay in the wrong field, the more a frustration builds that we cannot get from here to there. A creative block forms, changing those sticky strands into cement blocks. We are not going anywhere. We're stuck.

The longer we stay stuck, the harder it is to move. Discomfort builds as we start to believe in the 'I can't', losing sight of the 'I can'. Making the whole process plain uncomfortable. Turning our back on creativity, we walk away, never finishing our endeavour or even attempting it again.

HOW TO SHIFT

It's all about energy. I have worked with a number of blocked novelists who come to me in a state as they have deadlines and expectations to meet, and suddenly the book has dried up. That flow now seems so far away and the fear is great that they won't find it again.

Through hypnosis, I relax their mind, and then encourage their characters to come forward to write their own stories. They just need the author to tap the keys. In all cases, the block has released and the writing resumed. I have bounced the author back into the right (or write) field. Relaxed and feeling the creative energy, they get back on the wave, meeting the deadline.

To shift the block of this stuckness, you have to find your way back to the feeling department. Leave judgements behind and just create. The editing or corrective process comes later. Don't jump the gun. But do jump the stile.

The best way to do this? Soldier on. No matter how loud your critical troll is shouting, do your best not to listen. Keep pushing it away. Focus on the process in the moment rather than concerning yourself about its future.

When we are in the moment, we are at one with the process. There is nothing else but where we are and what we are doing. Watch your goal unfold. Step out of expectation. Allow the creative energy to do its job. Find ways to reinforce the feeling field.

I remember one novelist saying that before she began to write, she would sit on the floor and aimlessly play with a huge plate of sand. Just playing, nothing else. This was enough to shift her mind into the land of the creative flow.

Ask yourself:

- Why am I being so self-critical?
- Who led me to believe I wasn't good enough?
- Am I my own worst enemy when it comes to expressing creativity?

Judgement will not only stop the flow, but block it as well. There is always room for improvement, that's a given, but that's for later. Take it out of the picture. For now, just play and see what happens.

Believing you can't

The truth? What you believe, you do. If your stuckness strand resonates with 'I can't', you are firmly cemented. Don't even bother trying as you have already decided the outcome. Lack of self-belief holds you back. The only way to grow confidence is by doing. The more you do, the more you can do.

This is an interesting stuckness (and certainly a common one), for we are limited through not taking chances and closing the door to new experiences, new avenues of thought. The 'I can't' becomes the guard at the door, keeping the statist quo. Excusing our dreams away.

Of course, there is a lot we can't do, but only because we have yet to jump into the doing. Over and over again. I couldn't use a computer until, through perseverance, I gained the necessary skill, which continues to improve the longer I spend on it. That's the thing about confidence – it continues to strengthen. We cannot lose by learning. Knowledge enhances and expands doability. Unlike waving the 'I can't' banner, which excuses lack of doability. No need to worry about getting it wrong, failing other people's expectations, being more responsible, knowing where to go next. Those two words will always stop us in our tracks. At the same time, they'll fuel low self-esteem and lack of confidence. Doing creates growth.

A while back, I had the challenge of designing and delivering a new business course to a company. I was up for it. It was a signpost on the path I was creating. But hour after hour imagining, thinking, designing, writing and giving birth to another level in my work was soon taking its toll. All of a sudden, the energy stopped. I was blocked. Experiencing stuckness, I could no longer see the bigger picture. Didn't know how to draw it all together. It seemed so much bigger than me.

To get away from the stuckness, I went to lie down to see if I could figure it out. There, in the half light of the room, I suddenly saw in huge block letters, floating in the air above me, the words: I CAN'T. I hadn't even known that was what I was thinking, but at that point, I was seeing what I was thinking.

I wasn't going to have it. I imagined reaching up and erasing the 'T'. Now in block letters were the words I CAN. Then I wrote I WILL. I CAN, I WILL. Realising my mistake – 'I will' pushed the 'I can' into the future and the task needed finishing now – I erased it and replaced it with I AM.

There you have it. 'I can, I am' says it all. Back to the drawing board with these words playing loudly in my head, I did. I pulled it all together and went successfully where I had never gone before.

Of course, we doubt. We have no confidence when we have never used the muscles we need to use for something new. It is not in our spectrum of knowledge. Without anything familiar to draw on, we can feel it's too daunting. Just as I imagine the first time a baby pulls itself up to stand feels daunting. The baby will collapse down again, but it is in the pulling up that the muscles are strengthened. We learn as we go.

Believing that we can't justifies giving up and staying only with the familiar. But the familiar can entrap us in its stuckness. Doing what we've always done, we will get what we've always got. The stuckness of limitation.

HOW TO SHIFT

No rocket science here. To know you can, you have to change what you believe. Even if you don't feel it. Forward movement is born when you change the inner dialogue from 'I can't' to 'I can'. And the interesting thing is you feel it. Repeating 'I can, I am' did exactly that for me. I felt energised, inspired. The belief I had in my ability to create soared to the forefront of my being.

To support the negative means we do not grow. Fear stops us. Why support fear? You are a capable human being with a great capacity for figuring it all out. Give yourself that chance. Change the inner dialogue to the positive and I have no doubt you will rise to meet it.

Ask yourself:

- Who says I can't? Is it my voice or someone else sowing self-doubt?
- Why can't I?

Don't worry about the not knowing how. For the knowing is interlaced within the doing. The small child knows to keep trying to stand, as each attempt paves the way for their first step. Falling down didn't mean they couldn't stand. They'd done that already. Falling down gave them the knowledge and strength to know how to stand for longer, ready to move forward.

Lack of curiosity

We learn by questioning. 'What happens if?' 'Where will this road take us?' 'What is that thing?' 'Why?' But to prompt the question, we have to think outside the box. Outside what we know.

Lack of curiosity blocks us – keeps us stuck because we remain only within what we know to be true. We fish in the same pond. Hooking only what we've always hooked. But what about the unexpected, unknown, unexplained?

Curiosity is the root of all knowledge. We are spurred forward by a curious nature. Wanting to explore, discover, see more of what is and more of the why. When this delightful creative bubble filled with energy is lacking, we exist only in a familiar framework. There are no questions. No desire to find out – to go on the path of discovery. The mind stays the same shape it's always been. Staying locked in structure, not seeing the unusual. Preferring the trout to the mermaid supports stuckness.

The mind is like a muscle. Prompted to discover new avenues, it strengthens and expands. Which means energy finds new avenues of movement. There is a zest within questioning.

Lack of curiosity is a resignation. To lose the questioning of a child is to lose marvelling at the unknown. What if Isaac Newton, sitting under the apple tree, had lacked curiosity? Never thought to wonder why the apple dropped down? Fortunately for science, he was curious.

Curiosity is the forerunner of discovery. It encourages us to jump out of the knowledge box and step into the energy of wonderment. But with the box's lid firmly closed, not only does our essence of self get no chance to come out and play, to ride the waves of the unknown and the as yet undiscovered, there is no flow back either. Nothing gets into the box. Blocking that delightful energy of curiosity, we are starved of inspiration, motivation and, of course, discovery.

The strand of this stuckness is that lidded box, and we are in it. Humankind was not meant to have life all figured out, and then just shut down. This limiting and repetitive stuckness makes for unhappiness. Whereas the ray of curiosity picks us up and off we go. To new worlds, asking new questions with a desire to find the answers.

Remember Newton? Hmm...where would we be if he'd only seen the apple as an annoyance hitting him on the head?

HOW TO SHIFT

It's that box thing. Lose the lid, or at least prop it open. Your thinking will expand. No longer contained, it soars with delight.

Children are brilliant with curiosity. Always asking questions which not only surprise us, but make us think. Why? Because they want to know everything. They're tapping into the innate energy of curiosity.

By taking the lid off the box, you also take off the glasses of limitation. Then energy moves in a most delightful way.

Imagine viewing this planet through the eyes of a visitor. Be curious about what is around you. Not just the physical stuff, but on all levels. Why do you know what you know even though you never knew what you thought you knew? Ask the questions. For it is by asking questions you will find answers. Energy moves. Stuckness abates.

Ask yourself:

· Have I lost sight of everything but what I know to be true?

· What was I like as a child? What did I want to know, discover?

· How are my energy levels? Low?

· Am I suffering from stuckness and don't even know it?

Shifting perspective fuels and releases energy. The very act of asking the open-ended question 'Why?' sets the wheels of discovery in motion. And let's face it – there is so much out there to be discovered. Reclaim the eyes of a child and view the world with wonder.

Living through others

Why is it we have the hardest time seeing ourselves? I remember getting my hair highlighted from brunette to blonde. Although it was several shades lighter than it had been, for the life of me, I could not see myself with blonde hair. I had to ask others, 'Am I blonde?' Strange looks responded to my strange question. I was most definitely blonde – but not through my eyes.

It is really interesting, that invisibility cloak. Invisible to ourselves, we are dependent on others for feedback. It just makes sense, as does how much easier it is for us to focus on what others need to do rather than ourselves. We can see them. Especially those we love. We want the best for them. Want them to go forward and do the things we know they can do.

But at what cost? There is only so much room in the thinking department. While it takes effort to create visibility of self, it is far easier to become a support, backstage hand, director. When thinking of others, we don't have to think of ourselves. Discover who we are. Become more visible.

Think of the concept of the stage mom, pushing her child forward and living through their accomplishments and shining glories. Can you see how this concept supports stuckness? The stage mom is not on the page of her life. Absent from her, she remains invisible to herself. Maybe that is the driving force for the stage mom syndrome – visibility through proxy.

Like all stuckness strands, this one suits a purpose. Each strand weaves through the tapestry of life. But there is a sacrifice when we're only living through others – we end up absent from ourselves. And that would be a shame. I would hate to be at the moment of my last breath and wonder where I had been in my life. Sure, a strength for many, great at pushing others forward, but unknown to myself. The key to a fulfilling life is to become our own best friend.

HOW TO SHIFT

To help release this sticky strand of stuckness, you need to:

- Recognise you are a great coach – a natural
- Turn some of the energy towards yourself, helping you to go forward

When you shift this pattern loose, you shift the self-neglect stuckness. You know it is OK to think about yourself. Put yourself on the map. OK to change the direction of attention. For you are all important.

By only pushing others forward, you feed off their plate of accomplishments. But it's their plate, no matter how much energy you've poured into their life. Not yours. And what if they tire of you as their personal coach always knowing better? Where does that leave you? Invisible and rejected. Not a good script.

To shift this pattern, pull back on your energy and feed it into you. Discover you. It is a process of personal growth and awareness. I can now see the blonde me. But I had to work at it.

Taking off the invisibility cloak does require effort. But hey! You don't shy away from hard work. You're happy to do it for others, so do it for you. I have no doubt you will be the brilliant coach you've been waiting for.

Ask yourself:

- Why is it so important that others do well?
- Is it not equally important I find self-value? Am I feeding off the success of others?
- Where is the hunger for me?
- Do I believe it is wrong to think of me? Does that make me selfish?

Self-discovery is not an act of selfishness, it is an act of self-love. By balancing the energy of this pattern so it includes you, you will inspire and motivate others. You become a wise example with lots to share. Much more effective than just telling someone what to do.

Lacking hope

When lacking hope, we have no belief in change. This is what it is and will always be. We have a feeling of despair alongside acceptance of this stuckness strand. Something inside us has dimmed.

Unable to see the way forward, we believe the journey remains unchanged. We're living life on a low ebb, our thinking negative. Without the energy of hope – which is positive and uplifting – we feel a distinct lack in life. A resignation.

Without hope, life is tough. Despair is strengthened by the viewpoint of struggle. We feel isolated and accepting of separation. The puzzle is incomplete.

What is missing? The energy of hope. This energy is spiritual. It is the light which leads us safely forward in the times of great darkness.

Imagine a single lit candle. That is the light within that is there to connect and guide you. The candle sits alone in a candelabra, so you can add more candles as your awareness grows. With more light, there is less darkness. It not only makes it easier for you to see, but illuminates the path for others as well.

Connecting to all things, the energy of hope reminds us we are not alone. No matter how desperate the situation, the candle is always lit. When we lose sight, we feel lost in the darkness. Like we're wearing a blindfold, we do not see where we are or where we are going. Isolated, we shut down.

This is the saddest strand within the spectrum of stuckness. To move forward, we first need to allow the light of others to shine around the edges of our blindfold to help us not only see the blindfold, but take it off. For it is through this light we reconnect to the hope we carry.

No one was meant to go through life alone. The Heart fuelled by the light of another burns brighter. Energy moves.

HOW TO SHIFT

As with all stuckness, we prompt movement with self-awareness. But at some point in life, we've shut down. Perhaps knocked down one too many times, we just thought it best not to get up again. Not to try. We have lost our fire. By opting out (basically to protect ourselves from disappointment), we put on the blindfold, dimming the light within the energy of hope.

Without hope, despair grows. As protection, we shut the door on possibility. On the belief of positive change. Lack of hope pushes away any change. Without the energy of hope, we lack renewal. It's like winter all year round.

To shift, open up to help and be willing to receive it. For it is with another's flame that yours will be lit. And there is *always* hope. But seated in the darkness, unable to see either where you are or how to shift, like change, you may push hope away.

That's why the energy of hope has a failsafe. We can be affected by and realigned with the hope we carry within – our spiritual essence – through the warmth of another. To shift this stuckness, stop giving up. Ask for help to get up and stand tall once again.

Ask yourself

- Honestly – how negative am I?
- Does my fear rule?
- Have I lost self-belief? The belief that anything is ever going to change?

The flame of hope, innate to us all, fuels connection and possibility. Helps us to see the path forward and understand the path behind.

It is true the struggle of life can be overwhelming. With the pain too great, we shut down. Resign. But that light within our spiritual essence will not give up on us. It keeps knocking at our door. Our job? The door needs answering – opening. Letting in the light helps us see and pulls us forward. The strand broken, stuckness releases, as does our energy.

Pushing opportunities away

There are so many ways to push opportunity away. When we're caught up in this sticky strand, it's all about no – not yes.

No is not always verbal. We say no by not hearing an offer of support. Not responding to an invite. Not believing in possibility. Not believing we can do it and stepping up. Not seeing the potential. Not feeling the energy of growth, nor trusting the interest. When calling this stuckness into play, we are actually cutting our nose off to spite our face.

Why we would do that? Think about it.

Everything is energy. As creative energy, we are forging the path ahead. Opportunities do not come out of the blue. They are attracted to us because of something we want. A change requires us to grow. An opportunity is something wanting expression on a deeper level, and saying no (however we communicate it) stops the growth it offers.

Opportunity is the right set of circumstances at an appropriate time/occasion/moment. What's to lose? The fact that opportunity is knocking on our door says we are ready. And yet we don't answer the door. An opportunity offers change, a chance of success. Yet we turn away. An opportunity is solid. But makes us change. Fear barriers needing breaking.

How does this stuckness serve us? It is so much easier to keep our dreams as dreams. Just that. A bit shy of reality.

In writing this book, I so often saw myself. Different times. Different situations. Different patterns of stuckness. Years ago, when blogs were just becoming a feature in newspapers, I was offered one in the local paper. A vehicle into the world for my thoughts. But it meant I needed to expand my technical knowledge (not my strength).

I posted a few blogs, but when the help I needed wasn't forthcoming, I just let that opportunity slide on by. I said no because of my uncertainty. Lack of confidence. It is only now I can see what a great opportunity it was.

Pushing away opportunities is easy to do. All we need is an excuse or reason why we can't (good stuckness ingredient, can't). But is easy always the best path to take?

HOW TO SHIFT

Take one day and decide to say yes to everything offered. A cup of coffee when you are fighting for time? Say yes. Someone offering to critique your project? Yes. You've been feeling the impulse to do an online course and an email reminder just came through? Yes. Yes. Yes. Do it for one whole day. Don't worry about where it will take you, just be open to the journey. Then reflect back.

The coffee may have stimulated conversation that actually helped you save time. The review – always good to get another perspective. The online course set you on a fast track to a destination of desire. And if your yes is not working, then learn from that as well. Nothing is wasted in the lesson book of life.

Ask yourself:

- Is no my default when I'm offered something?
- Is my past peppered with opportunities I wish I had taken?

If so, be kind to yourself and learn from the nos. It is always good to have the slightly painful feeling of missed opportunity under your belt to make you more aware and open to saying yes.

Put your opportunity spectacles on and see the perfect moments in time and right circumstances coming your way. Changing perspective is ace at loosening the strands of stuckness. By saying yes, you ensure energy can now expand and strengthen.

Up in the air – getting unstuck

- Say yes – commit. Strengthening the commitment muscle increases productivity and grows confidence.

- A fifteen-minute walk in nature slows the mind and is good grounding.

- Organise – create order and experience the joy of doing.

- Commit to the doable (develop discipline). Do what you say you will do.

- Take on a challenge – be accountable. Push boundaries and commitment.

- Be spontaneous – take a chance. Learn to trust in the process.

- Develop a positive mindset – an essential tool for mind management.

- Get physical. Never underestimate the need for exercise, nor its importance for wellbeing. Plus, it feels so good.

- Repeat, 'I can, I am. I can, I am.' This stirs inner belief, fuelling momentum.

- Go off the beaten path. Travelling expands the mind, challenging self-limiting judgements.

- Eat well. Food is fuel. Choose wisely. The better the input, the better the output.

- Get creative – draw from the well (without judgement). Be inventive, curious and expressive.

- Value you. Put yourself more in the picture. By developing a supportive and loving relationship with yourself, you get to know the you in you.

- Play! Have some fun. We all need to lighten up. Laugher engages you with life. Releasing energy reduces stress and fuels positivity.

SIX

Sidestepping

Sidestepping. I instantly get a flashback to my horse. I grew up in a residential neighbourhood, so to get a really good run, my horse and I would have to visit the conservation land down the street. Without a doubt, every time we reached the point where we left the road and went down a small hill to the place where we could gallop flat out, my horse would do a sidestepping dance. Going neither forwards nor backwards, but prancing from side to side.

Finally, on strong insistence, I got her moving ahead. Once she did, she was in her glory – being able to run. Let herself go. So what was the sidestepping all about? Every time, I would have a bit of a battle getting her to go where she could really have fun. It wasn't like she didn't know what was around the corner. No. She knew each stone and pebble underfoot.

Of course, I also see myself doing the two-step side-to-side dance. Postponing doing what I really want to do. Sometimes briefly, until I give myself a good talking to. But other times, I deny myself the flat out run altogether. I'm lost in sidestepping until the desire, urge, want has been covered over with the dust of my hesitation.

Sidestepping is an extremely effective strategy for staying stuck. Remember, everything is energy. When we hesitate, pause, hinder forward movement, our drive dives.

Looking back, I never knew why my horse insisted on sidestepping. Fear? Wanting a battle of wills? A habit? Drawing attention to herself? Excitement? Not wanting to go forward? Could have been any number of reasons. And when we get caught up in the two-step dance, it is the same for us. In the end, what are we really doing?

When uncertain, we shy away from the very path we want to take, fuelling feelings of discomfort. We're like a fly in a spider's web, the strands of stuckness quickly wrapping around us, wasting time and energy with delaying or denying.

It is so easy to put the brakes on. Hesitation brings with it a multitude of reasons to support stuckness. But is this what we really want? Or, like my horse, is it a bad habit we are not even aware of?

Perhaps at this point, we need someone to come in and take control of the situation. Are we opting out of responsibility for the outcome of our actions? For many, the fairy tale in our minds supports how much easier it would be to have someone else take the reins in hand, showing us the way forward. Making us do it. Another flashback to my horse – maybe it is about power. When I had to be firm with her, perhaps there was a personal lesson there on taking control. We all have to feel confidence in the reins in our hands, otherwise all we'll feel is fear.

And do we really want someone else to make us do? That would be like riding pillion on a motorcycle, always having to go where the rider wants to go. Never getting to feel the full exhilaration of wind on our face. Sidestepping the power of potentiality.

I'm sure you know the script by now. This is the part where you see how much you sidestep. But it is one thing to see yourself doing it and another to discover the why behind it.

To release the sticky strands of sidestepping, we need to tap into self-honesty. By recognising our default setting, owning our behaviour, we can see the consequences more clearly. Every action creates a reaction, so if we want tomorrow to change, we must change what we do today.

So, why do we sidestep?

Lack of clarity

I remember being a passenger in a truck in thick fog. Visibility was just beyond the end of the hood. We were on a road with no option to pull off, no breakdown lane. All the vehicles just had to go forward and trust in limited vision.

But what if we don't trust? How can we follow a road that is hard to see? With little faith in our decision, we find that uncertainty, doubt and fear set in, as the lack of clarity strand grabs hold. The fog descends. Sidestepping, we pull away, locked in a holding pattern. Not going forward. We are stuck on the side of the road, unable to proceed.

It would be a heck of a lot easier if decisions provided us with a large spotlight so we could be assured each step of the way. But that's not how it works. When we make a decision, energy moves. We step on a path. Sometimes that path is easy and straightforward but not always. At times when it isn't, although barely able to see the way, like the driver in the fog, we need to have faith in the little view that we do have. We need to trust and pay more attention. When fear and doubt undermine our energy shutters, we find ourselves sidestepping instead of moving forward; we block ourselves through hesitation or abandonment.

Lack of clarity has a great deal to do with confidence, which only grows with experience. When we step onto a new path we need to accept the learning curve that comes with it but also to trust that with each step the path will be revealed.

Imagine you decide to climb a mountain. It's all new to you; you have no idea where your path will lead. Twisting and turning, it only gives you a brief view of the way forward. The occasional vista, a break in the tree line, allows you a view of where you are and perhaps where you've come from, but not necessarily where you are going.

That's the exciting thing about going where you've never gone before. It awakens you. All senses are engaged. You're invigorated; the climb becomes more important than the goal.

Stuckness sets in when we lack confidence in our decision-making. Clouding vision and fuelling self-doubt. Instead of relaxing in the knowledge that, by paying attention, trust will grow, the need to know (to see) the way becomes all important.

HOW TO SHIFT

We only get to know where we are going by the accumulation of the steps which we take.

The mind is a powerful thing, and just as it can push us forward, through fear, it can also reinforce confusion. Confusion can be paralysing, or an indicator we need to gather more information.

Pay better attention to the path. Don't just focus on the end game. Remember the path is part of the goal. Confusion comes with self-doubt. Check in on yourself. Use the eagle view. Look down on your life, rising above the fog to check out the bigger picture. At what point did the fog descend? And know that like any weather condition – including the ones of our mind – it will lift.

Shifting perspective, gathering more information, trusting in the part of you that wanted to climb the mountain in the first place will get you going. Knowledge and greater awareness have a way of doing that.

Ask yourself:

- Do I have to know everything before I start the unknown journey? How realistic is that?
- What information do I need right now that would quell uncertainty and lift my fog?
- Is this my pattern? Do I stop myself going forward by purposely creating confusion and submerging myself in self-doubt?

Step by step, that's how best to manage life. In this way, the path forward is revealed. The driver only needed to see the road just in front of the truck to make it through that patch of fog. When vision is obstructed focus on what you can see rather than fear what you cannot.

Jumping from one thing to another

Ahh, the butterfly mind. Flitting around. With lots of activity. So it may surprise you that this is an example of stuckness.

Remember, the stuckness web has many strands. It's made from different materials offering various strengths and durability. All suiting our needs.

With the butterfly mind, we flit about. Going here, going there. Doing this, that and the other, never settling. It uses a lot of energy. But how productive is it? You could argue that it works for the butterfly, feeding on each landing, but what is the point to us of fuelling up on petrol, can after can, with no destination in mind?

Just as we can feel like we have too little energy, we can also feel like have too much and not know what to do with it. Unsettled, we keep jumping from one thing to another, never leaving our mark. Staying caught in the web of activity.

Flitting does fuel interest. Unlike the strand of boredom, this strand offers change and input. But by jumping from one thing to another, we never stay long enough to sustain change. Imagine a large bedside book tower, the reader switching from one book to another. Dipping in, dipping out, they read all the books in bits rather than with the total immersion each story deserves.

What is lacking in this stuckness is being able to fully submerse ourselves into one task, one project, or the change we desire. It's all about the next thing, seeking further stimulus. We are never bored. But is that the motivation? Fear of getting bored? Yes, this strand has wings, but real trouble flying in a straight line.

Erratically changing energy direction reflects a mind which does not stop. Just as changing requires movement (hence the question 'Is this really stuckness?'), so does flitting from one train of thought to another. Imagine a field of butterflies going about their business. Now imagine an imposter trying to be like a butterfly. They could copy their actions, but for what reason? It isn't what they were born to do, so what are they doing? Wasting time and energy, which stops total immersion in one activity, goal, dream.

Without commitment to purpose, we never get to take that deeper dive. It is through following one train of thought or action that we allow the true project to reveal itself. The more we do, the more we understand what we are doing. All will be revealed. It is like reading one book at a time, totally immersing ourselves into the story instead of just skimming the surface. But if we start one thing, then bounce over to another and get distracted by something else, we end up with lots of could-bes and no completions.

When energy flits, it becomes movement for movement's sake. This stuckness sustains movement, but seldom clarity. And we need clarity for motivation. In fact, it is lack of clarity which robs the energy of motivation. With emphasis on the next thing, we don't even have time to think.

Ahh...is that the positive of this strand? It stops us thinking things through. Delving deeper. Sorting issues.

HOW TO SHIFT

We need to slow the pace of the mind. Meditation is a great way to still the mind by allowing thoughts to sail on by. Without getting into what we are feeling about that thought, and then having more thoughts and more feelings, we learn to detach. Accept that thoughts are like leaves on a river – let them float away.

Think of the ability to focus on one thing like a muscle needing to be strengthened. This is how you gain clarity and, with greater insight, know how to move forward. Plus, energy is more comfortable and relaxed. You could even learn to enjoy stopping.

Ask yourself:

- What am I afraid I will miss out on?
- Does chopping and changing work as a good deterrent to uneasiness or confusion inside?

- Other than more stimulation, what does flitting about truly accomplish?
- What is the adverse effect?

Movement does feel good. But remember the butterfly? They flit with a purpose. They are designed to change direction. It keeps them safe. Are you using constant movement and change to do the same? As long as you support what you fear, you also support stuckness. Even in movement.

Not knowing what to do

Imagine walking down a road, and suddenly the road forks with no signage. You have no idea where each fork goes or which one to take. Not knowing, you stop.

Now imagine walking down the road, and suddenly there are multiple roads branching off. There is way too much choice. How much easier would life be if you had a map to follow? Uncertain? Just look at the map. The map tells you where to go. How to get there from here. You don't have to take responsibility for the journey.

But life isn't like that.

Every step, change, action requires a decision. What to have for dinner? What kind of car to buy? To go out, stay in? For energy to flow, it needs to know what direction to go in. And with this strand, that's the challenge.

When the mind ping-pongs, clouding clarity, it feeds into uncertainty and lack of confidence, fuelling fear. Rather than feel the confusion, we stop. Leave the road. Maybe retrace our steps back to what we do know – safe in our comfort zone.

Although this stuckness energy supports mind management (we have stopped anxiety), it's in a negative way as it weakens decision making. Everything we do requires a choice – which next step to take. Pulling away from discomfort keeps us small. Sure, not knowing what to do or how to do something is a great excuse for not doing it. But how productive is it?

What it does is keep us where we are – stuck. Stepping off the path stops the journey. Energy must move to go forward. One foot in front of the other. Remember, we learn from doing. That's the reason we do things to grow. Doing builds confidence.

HOW TO SHIFT

The fuel of this type of stuckness is fear of getting it wrong and lack of confidence – not knowing how to do something. Both are uncomfortable feelings. So rather than experience the trap of uncertainty, unable to go forward, we slip back. Give up.

But remember the energy of change? We have to change. Energy must move, and if it is not going forward, it will build inside with frustration.

Undermining self-belief – belief in our ability. Which supports more uncertainty. Weakening decision making.

There is only one way to shift this stuckness and that is to stay with the feelings of discomfort. Don't run away. Pull back. Ignore or rationalise. Instead, accept you will feel a bit wobbly. Make those decisions. With perseverance, you will break through.

Directed energy knows where to go. Want porridge for breakfast? Your body easily moves to the cupboard to get the oats. It is that natural. Don't make any decision bigger than what it is. You are on a learning curve, so hang on in there with discomfort while trying to figure out what to do next. Perseverance is the key to the release of this strand.

Ask yourself:

- What if I moved the emphasis from what could go wrong to what could go right? How do I feel about just doing it?
- In the past, how easily did I give up on my dreams? Where did that get me?
- What if I learned perseverance? How much better would I feel about myself?

Sometimes we have to bring in serious self-discipline and soldier through, even when every instinct wants to pull back, retreat under the covers. It's so worth the effort. For when we commit to going forward, a backlog of energy surges forward with us, carrying us on a wave of wellbeing. Fuelling confidence. The map of life lies in the confidence of decision making and the simple fact that the more we do, the more we can do.

Focusing on everyday stuff

This is probably one of my favourites. Uncertain of the next step? Go do the laundry. The uncertainty goes away, and hey – the laundry needs doing.

Bouncing to the everyday doings is easy. We flow down a river, little effort needed. Tuck that paddle away as the tide of life does all the movement. We feel like we are accomplishing things, which comforts the frustration of not going forward. Stuckness awareness is held at bay.

But the problem with the everyday stuff is it is never done. A line can't be drawn under it. Clean laundry will get dirty. So the accomplishment is a bit of a low-level buzz. Rather a hypnotic flow where we do not have to think of anything other than what is right in front of our faces.

Just doing the small stuff keeps us on repeat, promoting stuckness. Making it easy to fall asleep in life. Houses have to be cleaned, dinners cooked, gardens weeded.

Let me share an example of this pattern which just happened to me (told you it was one of my favourites stucknesses). Being tired and on a deadline, I read the above and found myself struggling with how to take it forward. I felt I didn't have the energy. Couldn't get from here to there.

While I was staring at the page, my husband called out, having lost a lens from his glasses. So I went to look for it. I found it immediately, but the action of looking had me straightening the living room, which led me to the laundry needing to be hung out...

While this domestic dance of life carried on, I realised what I was doing. I felt stuck with my writing. Unsure. An energy pattern of unease. Looking for the lens gave me a reason to leave the struggle, and then hey! I was caught up in the rhythm of doing the familiar. Doing without thought and fuelling a feeling of accomplishment. While my writing needed thought, the small stuff picked me up and put me in a canoe, and there I was, floating down the river without a paddle. Accomplishing mundane tasks, I was getting away from the unease, confusion, uncomfortable feelings of giving birth to an idea.

Of course, I'm not saying that taking a break is bad when we're stuck. Facing the unknown. Creating something. Learning a new skill. In fact, stepping back into the familiar for a short while can enhance clarity. But not if it's overdone. When we're consistently doing the familiar at the expense of something new, something that moves our energy forward, it isn't positive at all. It's a stuckness.

Fortunately, because I am writing this, I clearly didn't slide into the stuckness of domesticity. Awareness shifted me back into the writing gear. It was a slow start, but now I'm taking the helm.

As energy, we fall into patterns. The dance of domesticity is one where we don't have to think. The repetition of doing keeps feelings at bay. Great way to stay stuck. But is that really what you want to do?

HOW TO SHIFT

Like with all of the many strands of stuckness, you have to see the pattern to change it. Notice what you are doing when you're swept into the dance of the small stuff. Clock your feelings. What were you doing before you suddenly had an urge to do the every-days?

In my example, I was struggling to gain momentum. Not a great feeling. The switch to doing the chores stopped that feeling, but you know what? Only while I was doing them.

Keeping yourself busy is a good way to ignore the inner tapping on your shoulder, telling you to get going and keep going. Turn up the commitment bar of accomplishment. Make it a priority. You know what? The housework can wait.

Ask yourself:

- What am I avoiding?
- Do I block myself by backing away when things get tough?
- How productive is this pattern?

Growth requires effort, and growing pains. But get through to the other side and your energy will give you what you need to go to the next step. It was through me seeing how I'd shifted from the discomfort of the unknown to the welcome sanctuary of the known that I was able to return to my desk and write through confusion and self-doubt. And when I did? A surge of energy swamped my uncertainty. Why? I had stopped running and faced my unease. Ridden the wave of struggle.

Struggle makes you stronger. Pushing forward strengthens your energy, like exercise strengthens any other muscle, while opting out feeds weakness.

Wasting time and energy

Isn't it amazing how fast time flies? Not necessarily only when we are having fun, either. We can be quite adept at ignoring the wings of time. Ever been pulled up short when you've run into a friend you haven't seen for some time? About how long it's been?

Yes, time can whiz on by, whether we choose to climb on its back and soar, or hang out below, watching TV, playing computer games, shopping or on the internet. Time does not stop just because we ignore it or waste it, which is an easy thing to do. Not wasting time requires commitment, focus and perseverance. Which may seem like hard work, but it's productive work. Wasted time creates unproductive energy. Holds us back as we ignore time and settle deep into the sofa of stuckness.

With this strand, we are focused on not doing rather than doing. We're just skating. Skating is pleasant, but if we skate on a small pond, there isn't anywhere else to go. Only around and around. Rather hypnotic. We are doing something, but keeping our energy well contained as life moves on by.

This sticky strand is like wearing stretchy leggings. So comfortable, that even when we're having a 'fat day', we are not bothered. Elasticity wrapping us up, flexing when we do, letting us take the lead, restriction free.

When we pull on the leggings of time wasting, it takes away the constriction of time. Instead of feeling the pressure to do, change, achieve, we are just plain comfortable. Thank you very much. Curled up on the couch, big bag of crisps, unconcerned what's on the box, we just keep on watching. And time passes. Energy lags.

Time is a structure created to help us do. Used wisely, it funnels energy forward. Wasted, energy seeps away. If we realise we are all living life on a deadline, maybe we will step up and value our time here. Change the leggings to more fitted trousers as an uncomfortable reminder we need to shift some energy.

HOW TO SHIFT

Recently, Apple created an add-on for the iPhone which tells us how much time we have been on social media compared with last week. Just giving us the heads up so we know. And it often comes as a surprise. When we waste time, we are not aware of time passing, which is why it is easy to waste.

But it is not only time we undervalue, but energy as well. I'm not saying that every minute of the day has to be of great value as we need moments of recharge. It is good to play. But if we are struggling with time, feeling there is never enough, then we are either giving ourselves unrealistic goals, doing too much, or throwing away quarters into the slot machine. The value of time is jeopardised. And that's the problem.

If time has no value to us, or not enough value, it is easy to waste it. But while we push it away, we also push away its structure. Structured time is a containment. We can do so much more when we work with it. The shift needs to happen in our relationship with time. We only have so much. How would we like to use it?

Using time wisely is not only about production, it also fuels energy. For just one day, keep a time journal. Clock what you do throughout the day. Be honest with yourself. You may be surprised how much time you are throwing to the wind.

Ask yourself:

- Is my relationship with time keeping me stuck? Always making me feel I don't have enough?

- Do I ignore time so I don't have to face the truth that time – time I will never have again – is passing?
- What could I do with more time? How could I structure my time better?

Awareness plays an important role in what you do each day. Stop excusing time away. Make it work for you. If you only get to see your family once a year, use that time well. Be real. Be present. Make it memorable. Not seeing the value of time will mean regret later on down the line. There is a payback in all action. Make an effort. Use energy to value time. Time to work. Time to play.

Procrastination

Saying, 'I'll do it after...', 'I'll just read a bit more, then...', 'I'll deal with that later, but first I have to...' does two things. It shifts us away from uncertainty and puts off what we don't want to do.

We all like our comforts. And being unsure about what actions to take is an uncomfortable feeling. Not wanting to do what we know we have to do is also not great. After all, who wouldn't rather read another chapter or two of a really good book than sit down and do the impending tax return?

Pushing a task away with rationalisation, we reassure ourselves that we will do it, but later. Even if it is something we want to do, but perhaps it's a bit scary – it's new, or we're uncertain how to proceed. By sidestepping into something more desirable (let's face it, even vacuuming is preferable to tax returns), we excuse ourselves, totally believing it will get done…

Let's look at the energy pattern of this stuckness. Caught in a procrastination loop, we are not going forward. But this is a great stuckness strategy as we really believe we will get around to whatever we need to do. Remember the joke gift plates, printed with the words 'round tuit'? Assuring the recipient that all the things they'd been saying they'd do once they got around to it would now be done. Because they had got the very round tuit they'd been waiting for. But the magic is not in the plate. The magic instead is in us. Using rational thought, we shift the time the task will be done.

But what is really happening?

Procrastinating moves a deadline around the corner so we don't have to see it. But we feel it. For we are all too aware of what we are doing. Or what we are not doing. Fooling no one, especially ourselves, is not so comfortable. Because putting off feeds discomfort, uncomfortable feelings don't go away. Dread, uncertainty, can't be bothered, to name a few, then support a negative attitude of not wanting to do what needs to be done.

Procrastination stops the flow. Excuses inaction. It is the taking of action which creates change. Remember that energy pressure – no matter how we excuse it away, it is still within. While this strand may seem to give us the power to ignore, in reality, it is taking away our power to achieve. Stuckness hobbles our feet. Why? Because in the doing, we not only get things done, we are also becoming more aware of what we can do. Confidence grows.

This is why external deadlines are so valuable. They are the finish line. The due date. They create a pressure to do. But when we tighten the reins, holding back, we create an inner tension which then needs overriding so we can do the deed. In other words, we create discomfort. Putting off what we need to do, or even want to do, we ensure our energy has no direction. It's not moving in a straight line.

HOW TO SHIFT

Work on accountability. Befriend deadlines. If you are avoiding doing chores or finishing projects, turn them into a game. Instead of saying, 'I need to get that done by…', reframe it and say, 'After I finish…I can then…'

Make a reward system. Put off reading your book until you've mowed the lawn. Tell yourself once you've finished, you can indulge in a delightful half hour of reading. You will enjoy your reading so much more by creating positive feelings of effectiveness and productivity.

Write a to-do list of everything you are carrying around in your head. Include within it things you want to do, but are perhaps uncertain how. It's the needing and wanting to-do list. Then pick out the simple ones. Cut the grass. Return a phone call. Little actions. Do one, then cross it out. Do the next. Cross it out.

Each time you take action without needing to be under pressure to do so, you strengthen your to-do muscles. Which is a great feeling as you gain more doability confidence and lose the horrible feelings which inevitably accompany procrastination.

Ask yourself:

- How am I not helping myself?
- Why do I put things off? What is the worst that can happen?
- Is it easier to stand still for an hour or move for an hour?
- Why do I make my life more uncomfortable?

As always, awareness is key. Hear yourself excusing life away or pushing things into the future. Rest assured that the pressure to do doesn't go away, but builds up within you, creating discomfort. Energy must move. The choice is yours. Will it be battering about inside, or outside moving mountains?

Not finishing

While visiting an artist's studio, I noticed lots of incomplete paintings lining the walls. Knowing the artist well enough, I asked, 'What's with all the unfinished paintings?' His reply?

'The problem with me, Cindy, is that I finish them in my head.'

Car boot sales are filled to the brim with projects which seemed like a good idea at some time, a possibility, but never reached completion point. Perhaps the people selling them ran out of steam, inspiration or 'stay-with-it-ness', their will to carry the project through dissipating. Maybe, like the artist, they finished the project in their imagination and lost the drive to complete it in reality. Or they ran out of time, materials, incentive, knowledge, concentration. There could be many reasons for lack of follow through. And now these unfilled dreams sit on a wallpaper table, waiting for a sale.

This is interesting.

While some people reinforce stuckness by not even starting, others thrive on beginnings. When we start something, we have already imagined it finished. Seen the possibility. Energy bursts through, fuelling take off. We're riding high on the wave of inspiration, but with no staying power or perseverance, our bright, vibrant creative energy will not be monitored and will soon dissipate. When that train leaves the station, the project is quickly neglected. Stored in the closet of things that need finishing. Eventually completely forgotten.

This stuckness strand is a bit of a red herring. Unlike other strands that frustrate, here our energy bursts out and is expressed, albeit briefly. Then it quickly retreats back inside until a new idea knocks on the door. It is a convenient way to stay stuck as at least we feel fantastic with the initial energy burst. But there's no follow through. No completion. Stuckness keeps us in a repeat pattern. We're a starter. But not a finisher.

I find it rather interesting how many stucknesses I can relate to as a highly creative person with an active imagination. Ideas fall down like raindrops. Each with the lovely feeling of potentiality. But like a coin has two sides, where I shine in creativity, I'm dulled in follow through.

I remember the exact moment this pattern shifted. I was in my twenties and full of ideas of what I was going to do. Lots of beginnings, but no finish lines. One day, I was telling my mother about a new idea. Fuelled with enthusiasm, I burned bright. But then I saw the look on her face. Really, it was just a shadow of a look. In fact, I'm not even sure she registered the shadow passing between us. But it was in that moment I felt the disappointment she carried as she knew I would never finish my amazing invention (or whatever it was that time). No words were said, but in that flickering of disappointment, I saw my stuckness clearly and made a promise never again to say I'd do anything I wasn't prepared to finish. I gave myself a rule to live by. And it has suited me well. Still that promise sits forefront in my mind. Keeping awareness present as ideas shower down.

It worked for me.

HOW TO SHIFT

The only way to develop follow through muscles is by commitment. Otherwise the strand of stuckness allows you lovely bursts of potentiality, quickly followed by disappointment. Maybe you can't see it, but others will.

To shift this one, you need to step self-discipline up a gear. Be firm with yourself. Make rules. Commit to strengthening the to-do muscles of perseverance, like you go to the gym to strengthen your physical muscles. Just like with any exercise, you are likely to be amazed at the change if you stick with it. And at your ability to make changes happen as well.

Ask yourself:

- How does abandoning projects serve me?

Be honest. Find the positive in the negative. Then you will know what you are really dealing with. It may be that if you never finish something, no one can judge it. Or there is no responsibility or accountability required. Always check into your fears as they are the holders in the stuckness web.

Then give yourself a manageable project to commit to. No excuses.

Being too comfortable

Oh, don't we just love our comforts? This is a big one for me. I take a bit of convincing to leave my warm, cosy bed, snuggled in my 400 count cotton sheets, on a dark and dreary winter's morning. I want to stay where it feels good. But life's not like that. We have to drag ourselves out into the cold. Face the discomfort of change.

When we get too comfortable, we don't want to change. Preferring to stay just as we are. Comfort can come in many forms. Lovely sheets, secure lifestyle, busy life, an easy existence. It is also in what we know and experience – the familiar.

Imagine everyone living in their own particular field. Surrounding each field is a border. Hedgerow, fence, stone wall – could be anything. Within the field are the patterns in our lives. Habits, the ebb and flow of daily life. This field is our comfort zone. It is where we hang out. Life happening as we know it.

As habitual beings, we are so comfortable in this environment because our life has settled into habits. We do what we do, and because we've done it enough times, we don't have to think about it. The conscious part of doing is taken out of the equation. Wake up, put the coffee on, wake the kids, make the breakfast while making their lunch and looking for the forms which need signing, run around looking for the forgotten bits, herd them into the car, off to do the school run. Back home, make another cup of coffee...Life becomes a dance of familiar movement.

We are comfortable in the dance. But we can get stuck in the dance as well. That's the tricky bit. Why? Change is an interrupter. It wakes us up. Threatens the comfort we've settled in to and, like having to leave those 400 count cotton sheets, it requires effort to change. The stickiness of this strand pulls us down deep into the comfy bed of life, drifting us off to sleep.

To acknowledge this stuckness, we have to be willing to shake our life up. Open to new experiences. Embrace changes which bounce us out of our comfort zone.

HOW TO SHIFT

Let's travel back to the field metaphor. What happens if a farmer never rotates his crops or move his cattle to another field? The field without the needed break begins to suffer. With repeated planting nutrients dwindle. Over trodden, the field turns to mud. Offering little to the cows.

It is the same with us. If we choose to live only with what we know, do what we have always done, our Spirit dwindles, as does our energy. Staying comfortable soon becomes uncomfortable. Irritability, boredom, frustration replace the once lush green grass.

To shift, we have to leave that cosy bed and be willing to put our feet down on the cold floor. Although a bit of a shock, it wakes us up and gets us going.

I am reminded of a time when I was in Wales, dancing in my place on the side of a steep hill. For 20 yards in front of me, there was a line of feathers being battered about by the torrential winds and side-sweeping rain. I was cold, wet, miserable, yet I held my space and I danced. Why? Because I had committed to doing a three-day Drum Dance with Joseph Rael, Beautiful Painted Arrow, a Native American Shaman from New Mexico. The ceremony is designed to dance our truth awake, and a big part of that process is discomfort. Throwing off the covers of comfortability. It's difficult. No food or water, and when we did get to rest, outrageous non-stop rain and high winds blew our tent down. Soaked to the bone, I danced. I wanted change, to grow, and to do that, I was there to shake myself awake.

Being comfortable is OK. We need to have ease. Being too comfortable excuses way too much, and in the end? It works against us. We need to push our boundaries. Explore new fields. Why? Because we are all so much more than what we know.

Ask yourself:

- When was the last time I did something out of my comfort zone?
- Really, how comfortable am I?
- What new experience is tapping on my shoulder?

The wonderful thing about stepping out of your comfort zone is you do not lose what you already have, and as confidence grows, you end up adding more acreage to your field. The more you experience, the bigger your field. The border? It expands, as does life.

Keeping everything the same

When I get anything new for my home – a couch, chair, lamp, vase, little or big – I place it in situ and it stays there. I only rearrange when something new replaces the old. Therefore, I was amazed at a friend who often shifts his furniture around. While he thrives on the thrill of changing his environment, I feel confident that I've already put things in the right place, so why would I move them?

Two different ways of thinking. Both OK.

But what happens when we try to control everything around us? Not letting any change happen. No rearranging. No new things finding their way into our home. Nor anything leaving.

Keeping everything exactly as it is, we build a fortress around our life, our environment, our time, our relationships, ourselves. It means that there is no room for the new. And although putting emphasis on the status quo means that we know what we know, do what we do, stay where we are, how realistic is that? Doesn't that get old?

Refusing change, pushing away growth, keeps us stuck big time. Why? Because as energy, we need to change. In denial of this, we keep our energy locked in, getting rigid in thought, word and deed.

Change is the pattern interrupter. I am sure that is why my friend loves stirring up his home. As habitual beings, we do not have to think about it once a pattern is established. It shifts down into the subconscious and becomes just what we do.

The great thing about being habitual is once an energetic pathway is established, we follow it with little effort. For example, brushing our teeth. I can't imagine anyone, unless they're using a new kind of toothbrush, thinks about how they need to brush their teeth. What to do first, up and down or side to side? No. The good thing about repeating an action is once we have created a neural pathway, we no longer need to do the driving. No longer have to think. Easy peasy.

Is that what this stuckness supports? Not having to think? Keep doing what we are doing? But that in itself creates a problem as we fall asleep. Patterned away, no longer actively moving, embracing, inviting fresh energy into our life, we become stale, as does our life.

Without room for change, change becomes a problem. Not allowed. Control becomes what we do. The downfall of control is it creates a dull life with a monochrome mind, which means our problems will always be just that: problems. Anxieties never get sorted, self-esteem bubbles at a low ebb. Sure, we benefit by the security of knowing everything is how it should be. But it's challenging in relationships as there is no room for the other person if we are the one in control. Rather hypnotic, this dance of sustaining. Change, on the other hand, brings growth and strengthens confidence.

This thread is similar to flypaper. Coated with super stuckness, it serves a purpose. But it's really not nice to have hanging around.

HOW TO SHIFT

This is tricky. To create change, we first have to see where we are. But when we are super controllers, we invest a lot of energy in control, so we don't see anything except what is out of place. Certainly, we don't want to think about change. With a lot invested in established patterns, we find it easy to pattern ourselves away. The security of sameness means we have no need to take chances.

To shift this stuckness, look just under the surface. Are you happy? Does the sameness of every day keep anxiety at bay? By doing what you've always done, you have no personal growth.

Change is great for mind muscle building. If there is no push for improvement, it's just like ignoring the physical muscles' need for exercise without challenge. Living at a low ebb, we are safe, but asleep.

To step out of this pattern of cement, stir it up a bit. Yep. Do something different. You can keep it small. Change does not have to be dramatic. Even driving a different way to work will wake up your senses as you are seeing new things.

That's it.

Your senses have to be awakened to loosen this thread. If you never go to the theatre – go! If you always do the dishes directly after you eat, leave them and go for an evening walk. Break up the patterns. Get out the big spoon and stir away. Stirring creates movement, mixes everything up just that little bit to give you fresh energy. The fresh energy fuels new avenues of thinking.

Ask yourself:

- Am I afraid of change? What does change mean for me?
- When did my thinking get so rigid? When was the last time I did something exciting?
- Was I always so patterned away?
- How does staying the same support me? But at what cost?

To change and step out of stuckness, you need first to see yourself. Each time you stir, your confidence is strengthening. Why? Stimulation awakens your senses, fuelling thoughts and feelings. Balance is key. Think of life as a recipe – a dash of control, a spoonful of what you know and always a glug of the unknown. By stepping out of the grey of sameness, you step into expansion.

An expanded life is anything but boring, for it has a mind no longer dulled.

Overdoing

The word 'overdoing' reminds me of a puppy flinging himself into a pond, excited to chase and retrieve a stick. Full of energy. Legs flying about, paddling a mile a minute, bouncing up and down. Creating huge splashes. The dog's head bobbing while he tried not to lose sight of his goal.

But then, all of a sudden, something must have clicked in the mind of the dog. For he calmed, and as he did so, his furious paddling dropped down a gear. All the movement on the surface of the water shifted down to his legs, creating a gentle wake. The dog, now able to see better where he was going, soon retrieved the stick, and just as calmly swam to shore.

As I stood watching the dog's transition from out-of-control eagerness to a gentle purpose-driven paddle, I realised something about myself. The dog's over-exertion reminded me of me riding a bike. Although able to ride, I never knew the enjoyment. It always felt like it was way too much hard work, and that's uncom-fortable, so not something I would choose to do. But it dawned on me the puppy had done something I had never applied to bike riding. He'd relaxed, while I used far more energy than I needed. So riding a bike was exhausting, with confidence always out of my grasp.

This is one of those weird threads where we unknow-ingly step into stuckness by using too much energy.

How can we be stuck when our energy is moving so fast? As with the puppy's eagerness or my lack of confidence (remember, we only get that from doing), we find we're driving in fourth gear where only second gear is needed.

Think about it. We overexert ourselves when we're unsure. Bull in a china shop ring any bells?

There is always the same amount of energy in the universe. It doesn't disappear. When we are consistently expending far more energy than we require, we create a drought elsewhere. Like burning the candle at both ends. Then we panic as the light dims.

Energy used properly matches the job in hand. Ever try to saw a piece of wood by pushing the saw instead of the movement of the saw leading your hand? It doesn't work so well.

Inevitability, when we overdo, we also overthink. Together, as well-known companions, they rob us of relaxation, dropping us down a gear. How does this keep us stuck?

By wasting energy, we create a lack elsewhere, leading to apathy. We can't be bothered. Too tired to do. But by never going the next step – relaxing into the process – we undermine confidence, which blocks us from trying.

HOW TO SHIFT

As I've said many times before, we have to see what we are doing to shift how we do it. Also, we have to own what lies behind the zealousness of getting the deed done. Like myself on a bike or the dog retrieving the stick, excitement, nervousness, uncertainty add more energy into the action. It's often difficult to see ourselves, but if we're known as a blusterer, a storm in a teacup, over the top or having too much energy for our own good, we need to listen and relax down a gear. Purposely take something at a slower pace, making it much easier to see what we are doing.

In my case? If I'd stopped worrying about what to do if a car came towards me, I might have had space in my head to notice the countryside around me while cycling. By slowing the whirlwind of uncertainty, we grow confidence.

Ask yourself:

- Do I go at things on super-charge? Am I matching the pace of my mind?
- How effective is that?
- How tired does that leave me?

Each task requires a set amount of energy to accomplish. Much like each recipe has a right temperature to cook it at. There's no sense paying higher gas bills and burning dinner. Regulation of energy means there is always enough to go around to fuel the change you've been wanting to make.

Sidestepping – getting unstuck

- Imagine a successful outcome. How good will you feel?

- Breathe – relax, focus on one thing, and then do it. Just one, and then the next.

- Get an accountability buddy. Support one another moving forward. Share dreams and make plans.

- Write it down – ask yourself how you will feel if you don't do it. And what if you do?

- Be spontaneous – just jump. Learn to listen and trust the part of you that encourages growth, not the part that supports fear.

- Communicate – ask for help. What do you need to know? Never be afraid to ask the question. Asking prompts clarity and knowledge.

- Finish one thing, then do the next. Develop action muscles. Always take note of how good completion feels.

- Relax, knowing it is in the doing that we learn. Creation is a process.

- Be firm with yourself. Take inner authority. Remember, if you don't control your mind, it will control you.

- Log your daily doings and notice time wasting. We all only have so much time – decide to get started. As always, awareness is key.

- Embrace discomfort – leave your comfort zone. Confidence grows, as does a new, expanded comfort zone.

- Do something totally new – shake up the neural pathways. Awaken. Don't let yourself fall asleep in life.

- Notice when you stop sidestepping and give yourself credit.

- Take power away from fear. Learn to recognise when you imagine disaster and re-imagine success.

Conclusion

At the beginning of our time together, and consistently throughout the book, I mentioned that to know where you are going, you first have to know where you are. Unless you read everything you come across, I would imagine you were drawn to *The Sticky Book Of Stuckness* because getting stuck is something you struggle with. How can you help but struggle when you are stuck? Energy must move, and when it is not, it creates an inner tension.

I know about that inner tension as I know about being stuck. It has to be one of the most frustrating energy patterns. Wanting to get going, but for whatever reason, not moving.

Awareness is key. When we are able to see what we are doing, we are much closer to undoing whatever got us stuck in the first place. But first we have to see ourselves. That cloak of invisibility I mentioned in Chapter Three can make it a challenge to see our part in creating our stuckness. It is always much easier to project it – the reason why we aren't doing, creating, changing, becoming – outwards. Perhaps those around us hold us back. Responsibilities stop us; health prevents us; there is not the money, time or place. Focusing on the excuses, not on the underlying reason for our stuckness, we have put the brakes on. As long as we support the blame or excuse the pattern, we will sidestep and not shift into drive.

But in all fairness, it is hard to see what we are doing, why we are doing the not doing. What is easier to see, as well to feel, is the disappointment. Disappointment is a funny thing. If we get used to it, we are truly stuck, the sticky strands of stuckness tying us down. Because disappointment can feel so overpowering, we stop thinking about it and just resign ourselves to living in a lower ebb of who we are.

To begin your journey, you have to know where you are. Looking up at the top of the mountain is really not going to get you there. The journey starts directly where you stand, and then it is one foot after the other. But what a journey it will be. In the process of movement, there is a feeling of deep relief and a surge of energy. Like your soul is crying out in celebration.

For myself, the writing of this book released me in ways I could never have imagined. It was a journey – just like climbing a mountain – and what I've asked of you, I also had to ask of myself. See where I was, not bemoan where I was not.

I've had to identify with my patterns, which blocked me time and time again. That's why it wasn't difficult coming up with thirty stucknesses (I have no doubt there are many more). Although there were some I couldn't relate to, others were so close to my core, I could have designed the tee-shirt. But the most important thing this book did for me was it taught me more about myself. Any journey in life is a process, and if we engage in that process, there is a richness to behold.

I did get stuck writing this book. But for the most part, it flowed through me, like I was just watching the keys dip down and up. All without thought. And where I did get stuck was when I had to experience what I was writing about. Life is like that. It teaches us every step along the way. Some lessons are hard to bear, while others are moments of profound insight waiting to happen.

I can laugh now, but those times the brakes drew me to a halt were uncomfortable. My inner troll was shouting in my head. But only as long as it took for me to see, hear, sense what was really going on. Then as I forced myself to get back to the writing, I had to laugh at the universe's magnificence, as well as its irony. What I thought I couldn't relate to became the issue which created the stuckness. How could I write about what I hadn't experienced? How real would that be?

Everything in life teaches us. It just depends if we are open to learning.

But we must be honest with ourselves. Not judgemental. Be kind to ourselves. For it is with love we relax, making it easier to allow change to happen. To embrace self-acceptance is like becoming our own best friend. All of us have a wealth of wisdom, knowledge, skill, ability and insight inside that adds value into the world around us. But if we only hang out around the edges of our potential, we never get to experience our capability. Or experience the joy of creative flowing energy. And it is a joy. Connecting more fully with ourselves is one of the best feelings we can experience. The us of us.

How do you start the journey?

- Without judgement, be honest with yourself.

- Own how you support stuckness.

- See all around its edges – how it affects your life and the lives of those around you and, more importantly, your sense of wellbeing.

- Take an energetic snapshot of how you are now, knowing you are changing by acknowledging the stuckness patterns you tie yourself up in.

- Feel the energy of restriction as you push the brake pedal to the floor, stopping forward movement. The frustration in your life is not because you can't do it, but for whatever reason you are deciding not to. Stuckness is not an outside thing, it is an inside thing.

- Be kind to yourself. Without judgement, it is easier to understand what you are doing to yourself. Without blame, it's easier to embrace going forward. When you apportion blame, you keep old wounds open and give power to the lack of awareness in others or situations beyond your control.

- Wipe the slate clean and begin another story.

- Keep the door to awareness open so you can see when you next shut down. It may be in a different way, but keep the stuckness alert button active. The more you see your behaviour, the easier it is to catch the stuckness before the glue sets.

When the strands of stuckness lose their hold, energy flows and life changes around you in a most glorious way. Why? Because you are actively responding to what your soul is calling. It wants you to ride the wave of forward movement. To respond to the dreams, desires, inner beliefs that have followed you from day one. Wanting to step up and into alignment with you.

When you only focus on what I call the outer world – the world of doings, of everyone else – you are missing out on truly being yourself. Just like each bee is born for its purpose, whether to be the cleaner of the hive, the collector of nectar, the hive air conditioner, the worker or the queen, you have a purpose. It is when you get trapped, either lost in thought, living up in the air or doing the sidestep of hesitation, you lose your way to inner discovery. You stay on the surface of your being rather than stepping in to and becoming the strength of who you are.

It is a process. I know. It's taken me a long time to get to this point. In all fairness, I have created and led a productive life which has reflected my path, but the writing? The real commitment to writing has always been a struggle. I wanted to, but never truly committed.

Desire is a grand motivator and fear a great builder of walls. Walls where we stay with what we know. If we stay with what we know, we stay where we are. The desire keeps calling, tapping us on the shoulder, while Mr Fear? He keeps pushing it away, building stronger walls to keep us safe.

Life is about learning, so safety is a relative thing. Every parent knows the swallowing of fear they need to go through to let their children experience newness. Having to stand by and watch them learn by falling down and getting up again. That is why there is no failure in life. Failure is how we acquire knowledge, ability and awareness to do better, and in the process, we get stronger.

I cannot emphasise this enough: it doesn't matter your age, ability, financial situation, health, location, for it is not of what is on the outside of you that I speak, but the inner you. Your richness of Spirit. You are so much more than meets the eye. While 'meeting the eye' is a surface experience, diving deep into self-honesty and embracing a non-judgemental relationship with yourself brings out the sparkles. Hope is reborn. Curiosity awakened. Muscles strengthen.

To live in the shadow of the self because no one has showed us where the light-switch is would not only be a waste, but also dim our view of the beauty which lies around us, and within. When there is not enough light to illuminate clarity, we end up believing in limitation. What we believe in is what we experience.

Don't settle just because you have difficulty in seeing the way forward. The way forward will always start from within. Why? Because it doesn't matter what is offered to you – if you are held in the energy pattern of stuckness, you will not accept it. It is only you who can untie the knots of stuckness. No one else. Nope. Not me. Not this book. Nor the wisdom behind it.

Only you can do it. Only you can begin that path up the mountain. First by seeing how far you have wandered from the path, then by picking yourself up and placing one foot in front of the other. The path and you have an integral relationship, and if you're willing, it will find you. The journey will continue.

It will happen for you. Of that I am certain. If you let go and forgive yourself, or anyone you feel is the reason why you are not fully you (although that is a handy excuse), you will release the most wonderful burst of energy. Sparkly stuff. And with it comes a joy inside yourself where each cell celebrates. Why? You were not born to miss out on yourself in your life. But to fully step in and stand up. Offering the world your uniqueness.

I am not talking about success in the world around you. For what is success? Years ago, a client asked me that exact question. My answer?

Success is when you are walking down the street and happy with what is in your head. If you have that, you have everything.

Success is the natural flow of you without entrapments to block and stuckness to entangle. Success is the joy of movement. Movement which comes from the Heart and expresses itself in its own way, however you express you. For when you do, when you truly express you, your Heart sings, your energy shines and all is well with the world.

Imagine that. If it were a mission for all of us to set our caps at doing one thing in life. Only one thing. Getting unstuck. How much better would we all feel?

Acknowledgements

The inspiration for any book starts first as an impulse, something intangible tapping on your shoulder. And although at that moment one feels, sees, believes in the potentiality of the idea, the tap, tap, tap has a very long journey to go before the idea becomes a reality. And like anything else, we do not walk this path alone.

Where do I begin?

Firstly, I would like to thank my good friend and accountability buddy, Theresa Harrison, who is always there to offer support, cheer me on, help me keep my focus. Everyone should be so lucky to have an accountability buddy. It's all too easy to avoid deadlines but not when you have a witness. Being accountable moves mountains.

A huge heartfelt thank you goes to Lucy McCarraher, Managing Editor of Rethink Press. She is a gift to me not only as my publisher but for her belief and support. She will always hold a special place in my heart as she was the first person to read my first manuscript and enthuse over its potential.

And then all those good people at Rethink Press, I thank you. Joe Gregory, Managing Publisher, for our brainstorming meeting, which helped me see a potential cover design and brought the book into focus. Loved that call, Joe.

For my attentive and positive Project Editor Kathleen Steeden, who held my hand throughout all the unknowns of the publishing process, the tone of her emails reassuring. Such is the connection that I feel like I know her, yet we've never met. I thank you.

Then there is my copy editor, Alison Jack. Editing is a profession I've never before experienced and it amazes me what the job entails. How does one hold an entire book in your head? Keeping the voice of the writer while making it more readable? I am in awe of her ability.

I thank my proofreader, Jo Holloway, for your eagle eyes and concentration. And of course, my cover designer, Natalie Kaaserer, who was able to blend my brief into the work of art it most certainly is.

Then there is my family, whom I thank for providing positive reinforcement. Especially my sister Dale, whom I refer to as my wise woman, always there to offer a lovely mix of common-sense wisdom blended with a dollop of creativity. As well, my brother, Jay, my bedrock of practicality, who pointed out details that never crossed my mind but were of great importance.

And, of course, Dad, thank you for teaching me not to shy away from hard work. And Mom, thank you for fuelling my creativity in so many ways as a child. Sadly, my dad is no longer with us but I am sure he will read this in his own way. And my mom? Years ago, she made me promise to write a book before she died so she could read it. As she's now ninety-four, I think I slipped it under the line. But Mom, here it is. I am thankful I could keep that promise.

To my husband, Nicholas, whose unwavering belief in my ability as a creative, healer and writer has never faltered. Even when wrapped in those sticky strands of not writing – he just kept reassuring me it would all work out. And he was right. I love you dearly and am always thankful you are my soulmate.

A huge thank you as well to all who enthused and reacted positively whenever I shared the title of this book. Each smile, nod and story gave me confirmation that stuckness is a universal challenge.

Last but not least, thank you to all my readers. I hope you, too, felt your sticky strands fall away. Getting unstuck presents an opportunity for greater things to happen. I would love to hear your stories. Please do connect with me on social media and share your thoughts.

So many good people – I am so glad and honoured that this was a path I did not walk alone.

Thank you,
Cindy

The Author

Cindy Hurn, known as the Metaphor Queen, has a knack for using images and storytelling to bridge states of consciousness. Born an intuitive, she is able to take a deep dive and bring to the surface light, direct and accessible concepts that introduce the spirituality of the higher mind.

With over thirty years' experience working with individuals and groups, Cindy is an expert in her field of personal development. As a transformational coach, she has an extensive toolkit to help open the door to awareness, from hypnotherapy, neurolinguistic programming, counselling, self-awareness training and executive mind management, to life coaching and intuitive readings.

Cindy's weekly internet radio show, *The Cindy Hurn Show: I don't want to know what's on your mind. I want to know what's in it. Your mind matters*, is now in its tenth year. With her deep perspective, strong inner connection and innate ability to traverse the landscape of the mind, Cindy shares techniques and metaphors supporting mind management while introducing the importance of the Heart. For that is what Cindy does: she thinks with her Heart. Always conscious of the bigger picture, she sees the mind as flexible, creative, embracing and connective.

Having changed the minds of thousands and with her audience ever growing, she has made it her mission to spread awareness through common-sense theory. Opening the doors to greater awareness, inviting in spiritual perspective.

Cindy's here to help. You can connect with her at:

- 🌐 www.cindyhurn.com
- f www.facebook.com /CindyHurnTransformationalCoach
- 𝕏 @CindyHurn
- in www.linkedin.com/in/cindyhurn
- 🎤 www.cindyhurn.com/services/the-cindy-hurn -show
- 📷 Cindy_Hurn

Lightning Source UK Ltd.
Milton Keynes UK
UKHW020633240122
397612UK00005B/291